Journey with the Expanded Rosary

Experience the Mysteries for Each Day of the Week

A Devotional Guide

Journey with the Expanded Rosary

Experience the Mysteries for Each Day of the Week

A Devotional Guide

Rich Melcher

LEONINE PUBLISHERS
PHOENIX, ARIZONA

Copyright © 2016 Richard Corsair Melcher

All rights reserved. No part of this book may be reproduced or transmitted in any form or by any means, electronic or mechanical, including photocopying, recording, or by any information storage or retrieval system now existing or to be invented, without written permission from the respective copyright holder(s), except for the inclusion of brief quotations in a review.

The Scripture citations used in this work are taken from the *Saint Joseph Edition of the New American Bible*, revised edition, copyright © 2011, by Catholic Book Publishing Corporation, New Jersey.

Cover design by Rick McCoy.

Published by Leonine Publishers LLC
Phoenix, Arizona
USA

ISBN-13: 978-1-942190-22-6
Library of Congress Control Number: 2015959418

Printed in the United States of America
10 9 8 7 6 5 4 3 2 1

Visit us online at www.leoninepublishers.com
For more information: info@leoninepublishers.com

Contents

Foreword by Bishop Donald Hying. vii
Introduction to the T.E.R.M. Rosary 1

Section I
T.E.R.M. Mystery Biblical Citations and Reflections

Chapter 1
Mysteries of the Heart 9

Chapter 2
Mysteries of the Miracles 18

Chapter 3
Prince of Peace Mysteries 30

Section II
Reflections for the Traditional Mysteries

Chapter 4
The Joyful Mysteries 44

Chapter 5
The Luminous Mysteries 55

Chapter 6
The Sorrowful Mysteries 67

Chapter 7
The Glorious Mysteries 82

Section III
Basics of the Rosary

Chapter 8
The Basics of the Rosary 98

Foreword

Rich Melcher offers us a new way to pray a traditional Catholic devotion in his book, *Journey with the Expanded Rosary*. His very personal reflections, filled with experiences of grace, friendship, pain, struggle, and ultimately faith, remind us that the story of Jesus Christ and His Mother Mary is fundamentally the narrative of our own lives.

The meaning of our existence, with its myriad relationships, encounters, joys and sorrows, hopes and disappointments, finds its fulfillment in the Incarnation, life, ministry, death and resurrection of Christ. This book fills in the details between the big events, leading us to ponder the glittering facets of Jesus' Heart: peacemaking, healing, and numerous moments of transformation in the lives of those He touched.

Without abandoning the traditional form of the rosary, Melcher opens us up to the evocative power of this rich form of prayer which is designed to lead us into fruitful meditation on the lives of Jesus and Mary. The author models for us in these transparent vignettes of personal experience, which are profoundly vulnerable and self-revelatory, how to make the fundamental and needed connections between the life of the Son of God and our own.

At times, we are tempted to think that the Scriptures constitute a story about somebody else living somewhere else, far away and irrelevant to our time and our experience. Rich Melcher helps us to bridge this divide and invite the Lord into the complex and messy reality of daily life. Amid friendships and work projects, dirty dishes and sports, heartbreaking setbacks and moments of joyful connection, the Lord breaks into our hearts and our lives, to heal, love, forgive, and transform us.

I recommend *Journey with the Expanded Rosary* for everyone who seeks to make their relationship with Jesus and Mary come alive in living color, to connect the traditional rosary mysteries with the mysteries of our own lives, to creatively imagine ourselves in the deepest part of our identity, as beloved children of the Father and as actors in the great drama of salvation. Use this beautiful book to fall ever more deeply in love with the Lord as we make this challenging yet beautiful pilgrimage to the glory of the Father's house.

Bishop Donald Hying
Diocese of Gary, Indiana

Introduction to the T.E.R.M. Rosary

What if you had a form of personal prayer that encouraged you to meditate on thirty-five scenes from the life of Jesus Christ as portrayed in the Bible? And in visualizing the life of Jesus, what if this method of prayer enabled you to find yourself living out His example of love and mercy more fully? What if you could pray a renewed form of an ancient prayer that could enliven your spiritual life and allow you to receive ample graces from the Holy Spirit?

What is this prayer?

It is the "T.E.R.M. rosary." What is the T.E.R.M. rosary? We'll get to that in a moment.

But first, the original rosary, which dates back to AD 1214, is a grouping of daily prayers which are prayed using fifty-nine beads and a crucifix as a guide.

There are five "mysteries" to be meditated upon each day. A *mystery*, in this sense, is a scene from Jesus' life (or His mother Mary's) that depicts a specific dramatic event in His (or her) life—from His baptism, to the Agony in the Garden, to the Resurrection.

For over thirty-five years as a "cradle Catholic" (meaning a Catholic since birth), I've known *how* to pray the rosary. (Just like knowing *how* to play chess—knowing the movements of the pieces—but without any strategies.) Yet I've only been praying it on a regular basis since August 16th, 2008. Why that particular date?

On that sunny summer day, while walking through a Target store parking lot near my home in Milwaukee, Wisconsin, I came across a likeness of Mary, Jesus' mother, that I had never seen before. Her colorful image was on a piece of thin cardboard, about the size of a credit card. As I picked it up off the hot pavement, I realized that it was one of those "dangly things" that hangs from the rear-view mirror of a car. It was likely that it had been lost or perhaps recklessly tossed out of the window of a passing car. Holding the card in my hands, I pondered, "Which Mary is this, and what culture does this image represent?"

I took the holy card home to my wife, Sandra, who immediately identified the picture as "Our Lady of Guadalupe." This image depicts an apparition (appearance) of Mother Mary in AD 1531, in Mexico City.

Discovering the Our Lady of Guadalupe card that afternoon inspired me to pick up one of my many rosaries and begin to pray that twenty-to-twenty-five-minute devotion, which I did each day for the next one and a half years.

Yet by the summer of 2009, I had become somewhat weary of praying the rosary. You see, with the rosary, there is a great amount of repetition. My personal challenge was not that of repeating the "Hail Mary" over and over each time I prayed the rosary. It was the repetition of the three original sets of mysteries: The "Joyful," the "Sorrowful," and the "Glorious." And since one of the main purposes of the rosary is to meditate on the life of Christ, this repetition significantly diminished my spiritual creative imagery, thereby reducing its spiritual potency in my prayer life.

So, with much prayer, and with guidance from the Holy Spirit, I decided to create three new sets of mysteries, one set for each repeated day: Tuesday, Wednesday, and Saturday. (Since there are only three sets of mysteries and yet seven days of the week, some mysteries are prayed more than once during the week). I scoured the New Testament and discovered fifteen additional scenes from Jesus' life to illuminate what I call the

"Tri-Expanded Rosary Mysteries"—"Tri-Expanded" referring to the three new sets. (Tri-Expanded Rosary Mysteries can be abbreviated to the acronym T.E.R.M.)

Using the familiar fifty-nine rosary beads and a crucifix, these additional mysteries enhance the original three sets along with the fourth set, the "Luminous Mysteries," which were introduced in 2002 by Pope John Paul II, and which are now prayed on Thursdays. The T.E.R.M. mysteries, along with the traditional mysteries, create the T.E.R.M. rosary. It offers those who pray the traditional rosary a bright, refreshing opportunity to pray additional mysteries each day of the week.

The T.E.R.M. rosary adds the T.E.R.M. mysteries, which are:

> Mysteries of the Heart (Prayed on Tuesdays)
>
> Mysteries of the Miracles (Prayed on Wednesdays)
>
> Prince of Peace Mysteries (Prayed on Saturdays)

The citations for each new mystery are strictly scripture-based, quoted directly from the New American Bible (with one exception). Also, each is accompanied by T.E.R.M. mystery reflections that encourage those praying the T.E.R.M. rosary to meditate more deeply on the life of Christ (chapters 1–3). Included in the text are reflections for the twenty traditional mysteries of the rosary (chapters 4–7) which bring opportunities for even more spiritual exploration. The final chapter adds a brief instruction for the praying of the rosary to assist in praying the T.E.R.M. rosary.

As mentioned earlier, one of the main purposes of the rosary has always been to graphically envision the life and times of Jesus Christ. The vivid images of the T.E.R.M. rosary can help people pray more faithfully, by reverently imagining fifteen new scenes of His life (totaling thirty-five mysteries). Visualization is the key. When we envision significant things in our lives, we move toward them. And what Christian wouldn't like to move into greater alignment with the ways of Jesus?

Imagine the joy and fulfillment of experiencing spiritually-transformative moments in your life—inspired by the life of Jesus. This is what the T.E.R.M. rosary offers. I encourage you to explore the T.E.R.M. rosary to see how it can bring more meaning and spiritual enrichment into your life.

In Christ,

Rich Melcher

T.E.R.M. Rosary

The T.E.R.M. rosary adds three sets of five mysteries to the original four sets of the Holy Rosary. The "traditional" mysteries include the Joyful, Sorrowful, Luminous, and Glorious Mysteries. A schedule of all the mysteries together is on the following page.

Traditional and T.E.R.M. Mysteries Schedule

Day	1st Mystery	2nd Mystery	3rd Mystery	4th Mystery	5th Mystery
Mondays **JOYFUL** (Traditional)	The Annunciation	The Visitation	The Nativity	The Presentation	Finding the Jesus in the Temple
Tuesdays **HEART** (T.E.R.M.)	Clean Heart	Aware Heart	Broken Heart	Joyous Heart	Compassionate Heart
Wednesdays **MIRACLES** (T.E.R.M.)	Jesus makes the lame man walk	Jesus feeds the 5,000	Jesus makes the blind man see	Jesus cures the leper	Jesus casts out the evil spirits
Thursdays **LUMINOUS** (Traditional)	The Baptism of the Lord	The Wedding Feast at Cana	The Proclamation of the Kingdom	The Transfiguration	The Institution of the Eucharist
Fridays **SORROWFUL** (Traditional)	The Agony in the Garden	The Scourging at the Pillar	The Crowning with Thorns	The Carrying of the Cross	The Crucifixion
Saturdays **PRINCE OF PEACE** (T.E.R.M.)	Blessed are the peacemakers	Peace! Be Still!	Peaceful prayer in the deserted places	Peaceful patience	Peace be with you
Sundays **GLORIOUS** (Traditional)	The Resurrection	The Ascension	The Descent of the Holy Spirit	The Assumption of Mary	The Coronation of Mary

Section I
T.E.R.M. Mystery Biblical Citations and Reflections

Below, each T.E.R.M. mystery is identified in the Bible and enlivened by original reflections, written by the author, to provide insight and information to help readers get the most out of their T.E.R.M. rosary prayer time. These reflections can be applied in many fruitful ways:

1. Read one reflection for one of the five mysteries of the day
2. Read more than one reflection for that mystery
3. Read one reflection for each mystery of the day
4. Read a small section of a reflection and visualize it
5. Any number of combinations using the mysteries for the day

Some may want to read the reflection(s) before praying the T.E.R.M. rosary, or intermittently during the rosary, or afterwards. Also, some may just want to enjoy a number of reflections from the T.E.R.M. mysteries or the traditional mysteries.

The purpose of these reflections is to lead you into a prayerful interior life, while also encouraging new and possibly unfamiliar ways of looking at the events of Jesus' life. Thus, through the T.E.R.M. rosary and the reflections, you may enjoy a fuller and richer relationship with Jesus Christ.

Chapter 1
Mysteries of the Heart

Prayed on Tuesdays

1. Clean Heart
2. Aware Heart
3. Broken Heart
4. Joyous Heart
5. Compassionate Heart

Biblical Citations

*1) **Jesus' clean heart**: John the Baptist cries out "Repent!"*
~Matthew 3:1-2~

"In those days John the Baptist appeared, preaching in the desert of Judea [and] saying, 'Repent, for the kingdom of heaven is at hand!'"

*2) **Jesus' aware heart**: God proclaims,*
"You are my beloved Son…"
~Mark 1:10-11~

"On coming up out of the water he saw the heavens being torn open and the Spirit, like a dove, descending upon him. And a voice came from the heavens, 'You are my beloved Son; with you I am well pleased.'"

*3) **Jesus' broken heart**: Jesus is perturbed and troubled*
over Lazarus' death. "And Jesus wept."
~John 11:33-35~

"When Jesus saw her weeping and the Jews who had come with her weeping, he became perturbed and deeply troubled, and said, 'Where have you laid him?' They said to him, 'Sir, come and see.' And Jesus wept."

*4) **Jesus' joyous heart**: Jesus loves the children…*
"Let the children come to me…"
~Mark 10:13-16~

"And people were bringing their children to him that they might touch him, but the disciples rebuked them. When Jesus saw this he became indignant and said to them, 'Let the children come to me; do not prevent them, for the kingdom of God belongs to such as these. Amen, I say to you, whoever does not accept the kingdom of God like a child will not enter it.' Then he embraced them and blessed them, placing his hands on them."

> 5) ***Jesus' compassionate heart***: *The woman caught in adultery…"Neither do I condemn you…"*
> *~John 8:7, 9-11~*

"'Let the one among you who is without sin be the first to throw a stone at her.' And in response, they went away, one by one, beginning with the elders. Then Jesus straightened up and said to her, 'Woman, where are they? Has no one condemned you?' She replied, 'No one, sir.' Then Jesus said, 'Neither do I condemn you. Go, [and] from now on do not sin anymore.'"

Mysteries of the Heart Reflections

CLEAN Heart

A. "A clean heart create for me, God; renew within me a steadfast spirit." (Psalm 51:12)

Isn't this what John the Baptist was crying out in the desert? We must look at our lives, examine ourselves, and truly see who we are and what is within us—the good and the not-so-good.

The mystery of the Clean Heart emphasizes how John called out "Repent!" and "Prepare ye the way of the Lord!" to awaken others to a world beyond his teachings—to the world of the Good News. John truly heralded the coming of Jesus by challenging God's people to clean up their lives and "put their houses in order," and he baptized them (as scripture foretold) so that when Jesus came, they would be prepared.

In what particular ways are you called to have a clean heart? Is it in your dealings with your job, where you may be tempted to cut corners or skim a little off the top? Or is it in your relationships with loved ones, where you may not be willing to put effort into taking risks to build intimacy? To be "blameless before God" is a pretty tall order—but one we are called to conform to. It is a challenge only Christ can help us attain. It *is* Godliness. "Give me a clean heart, and I'll follow Thee," proclaims the old gospel spiritual—and what can be more freeing than a clean heart, on the road to God's glory?

* * * * * * * * * * *

B. In Leviticus 13:45–46, it reads, "The garments of one afflicted with a scaly infection shall be rent and the hair disheveled, and the mustache covered. The individual shall cry out, 'Unclean, unclean!' As long as the infection is present, the person shall be unclean."

Leprosy may no longer be common in our society today, but there are other kinds of great sufferings. Self-stigma can be the worst type of stigma because it occurs inside the heart and mind. We don't go around calling out, "Unclean! Unclean!" But even without spoken words, this can be an inner cry, a prejudice of the soul, a brokenness of heart.

Jesus challenged people, and healed many of them. He cleaned their hearts, as He does ours today. But we need to cooperate with such healing. We need to stop tearing ourselves down, and to stop being our own worst enemy. Jesus told the leper, "Be made clean!" And the belief that it could be done brought the leper back to health. We can ask for a clean heart, and Jesus will make it so.

AWARE Heart

A. Jesus was found safe in the temple at age twelve, after having been lost for three days. Amazingly, He was fully aware that He was God's son at that moment. He very clearly told His mother and Joseph, "I must be about my Father's house."

A supreme affirmation came to Him at His baptism eighteen years later when the clouds opened up and the Holy Spirit came down upon Him in the form of a dove. Then He heard those words, "You are my beloved Son; with you I am well pleased." This was not a wake-up call for Jesus, but merely a reminder that, indeed, He was the Son of God.

In this awareness, He headed forth with courage and resolve, to teach and heal, to preach and comfort the poor and the sick—to be the Good Shepherd, and, paradoxically, the Lamb of God.

* * * * * * * * * * * *

B. When you are aware of who you are, you can do marvelous things. For many people, much of life is spent trying to figure out who they are. Some may wonder, *what are my morals, my preferences, my convictions, my innermost thoughts?*

Jesus taught us how to be aware. Have you experienced His presence when you are trying to make a big decision? He helps us believe in ourselves. He knew. He knew His mission and His obstacles, and he forged ahead no matter the odds of successful outcomes. Jesus has an *aware* heart, and teaches us how to seek the same.

BROKEN Heart

A. Jesus lost one of His best friends, Lazarus.

How many of us have found ourselves unable to be present for another in his or her time of need because of pressing responsibilities? Did He weep over His loss, or possibly over the loss of those around Him? He heard the cry, "Why did you not come earlier—my brother would still be alive!"

And Jesus wept.

This is one of the shortest phrases in the whole Bible. And it came at a time of deep grief for Jesus, where there was nothing more to say. He had been away. But He asked His Father for a manifestation of His power. And His Father granted it. Death would not prevail—the Love of God would win in the end. And Lazarus was raised.

* * * * * * * * * * *

B. It was supposed to be one of the most joyful moments of His life—the first proclamation of the Good News. It started out well enough, with Jesus reading from the book of Isaiah, where the prophet speaks about "restoring sight to the blind, freeing captives, and making the lame walk." Those listening looked at Him in awe when He proclaimed that this prophecy was coming to life at that moment.

Then He went on and shocked them by saying that some Gentiles had deeper faith than they did. So they dragged Him out of the synagogue to the edge of a cliff, intending to throw Him off. But he walked through them and escaped.

What a welcome! This reaction was an explosive one, and a sorrowful one, for Jesus. He could see what He was up against, and it wasn't pretty. Jesus and His message had taken a hit immediately. Where would this lead to?

JOYOUS Heart

A. Is there any greater joy than spending time with a child? Jesus experienced this: "And people were bringing their children to him that he might touch them…" (Mark 10:13) Jesus was grieved by His apostles when they insisted the children go away! He was probably having the best time of His week—or month—enjoying the company of these little ones. And why? Because children often exude pure joy, and stir up joy within us.

I was recently honored to spend a full day with my nine-year-old granddaughter and it was one of the most joyful events of my life. She is so inquisitive, curious, and loving (and precocious) that she allowed the kid in me to come out and play. This may sound simplistic to others—maybe even ridiculous—but walking around downtown Chicago for five hours with her was a huge event for me. I assure you, it was better than any Broadway play, home-team Super Bowl victory, or birthday surprise party. At age nine, my granddaughter showed me the town—her hometown—her school, the downtown public library, the stores, and more. And we both experienced God's joy. A beautiful thing!

The gift of Love shared with a child is one of the most precious things on earth, and Jesus affirmed this.

* * * * * * * * * * * *

B. After reading Mark 10:13–16 a few months ago, just before retiring for the evening, I came to a realization. I thought about what Jesus had said: "Whoever does not accept the kingdom of God like a child will not enter it." A seed that had rested inside me, untouched, for many years, broke open and sprouted. How many times in my life had I heard, "You need to have a childlike faith"? Countless times!

But suddenly, my eyes were opened. It was a turning point in my life. It became clear to me that my faith had been wavering because I had so many questions, and so few answers. I didn't want to be wrong, but I didn't want others to be wrong, either. Childlike faith—this was all I needed. I didn't have to have all the right answers. I didn't have to know how I felt about all the big issues in life. I was simply called to believe, to trust, to have faith. And no matter how astute or learned or spiritually advanced I could be, I would still be far below the depths and heights of God's knowledge. I saw that I was just an ordinary person with ordinary concerns.

With childlike faith comes childlike joy. This gift was given to me that night because I no longer had to put on a masquerade of being learned. I could simply be MYSELF. This was so refreshing and invigorating that I can still feel the freedom that I experienced at that moment. It is a part of me now. Thank You, God, for giving me childlike faith!

COMPASSIONATE Heart

A. We all get caught up in our sins, in one way or another. Jesus has a special way of bringing this to our attention. It is called "conscience." He touched the heart of the woman caught in adultery by appealing to her conscience.

She was caught in a web of social impurity. Where was the man who had been involved? Why was he not brought forth to be stoned? Even today a pregnant woman can be abandoned while the man runs free. It is unjust.

Jesus saw in and through and around all of this. He knew the woman was being used as a scapegoat and that she was not the only one to blame. Blame was also upon all those who wanted to stone her. And He revealed this to them: "Let the one among you who is without sin be the first to throw a stone at her."

* * * * * * * * * * * *

B. Another place in the Bible where Jesus showed His compassionate heart was when He met the Samaritan woman at the well. He wasn't even supposed to be talking to her. Jews didn't talk to Samaritans. They also did not speak with strange women. But Jesus didn't have a bucket, so He asked her to draw up some water for Him, and then went on to offer her "living water." She did not understand that He was talking about Himself. But when He told her that she had had six husbands and was not even married to the man she was then living with, she ran back to her people and exclaimed that He knew everything about her.

This proclamation brought many people to Him, and He gave them all "living water." His compassion for one became salvation for many.

Chapter 2
Mysteries of the Miracles

Prayed on Wednesdays

1. Jesus makes the lame man walk
2. Jesus feeds the 5,000
3. Jesus makes the blind man see
4. Jesus cures the leper
5. Jesus casts out the evil spirits

Biblical Citations

1) Jesus makes the lame man walk...
"pick up your mat and go home..."
-Mark 2:9-12-

"'Which is easier, to say to the paralytic, "Your sins are forgiven," or to say, "Rise, pick up your mat and walk"? But that you may know that the Son of Man has authority to forgive sins on earth,'—he said to the paralytic, 'I say to you, rise, pick up your mat, and go home.' He rose, picked up his mat at once, and went away in the sight of everyone."

2) Jesus feeds the 5,000...
"Give them some food yourselves..."
-Mark 6:34-42,44-

"When he disembarked and saw the vast crowd, his heart was moved with pity for them, for they were like sheep without a shepherd; and he began to teach them many things. By now it was already late and his disciples approached him and said, 'This is a deserted place and it is already very late. Dismiss them so that they can go to the surrounding farms and villages and buy themselves something to eat.' He said to them in reply, 'Give them some food yourselves.' But they said to him, 'Are we to buy two hundred days' wages worth of food and give it to them to eat?' He asked them, 'How many loaves do you have? Go and see.' And when they had found out they said, 'Five loaves and two fish.' So he gave them orders to have them sit down in groups on the green grass. The people took their places in rows by hundreds and by fifties. Then, taking the five loaves and the two fish and looking up to heaven, he said the blessing, broke the loaves, and gave them to [his] disciples to set before the people; he also divided the two fish among them all. They all ate and were satisfied. ...Those who ate [of the loaves] were five thousand men."

3) Jesus makes the blind man see…
*"The man called Jesus made clay and anointed my eyes—
and I was able to see."*
~John 9:5-7~

"'While I am in the world, I am the light of the world.' When [Jesus] had said this, he spat on the ground and made clay with the saliva, and smeared the clay on his eyes, and said to him, 'Go wash in the Pool of Siloam' (which means Sent). So he went and washed, and came back able to see."

4) Jesus cures the leper… "I do will it. Be made clean."
~Mark 1:40-42~

"A leper came to him [and kneeling down] begged him and said, 'If you wish, you can make me clean.' Moved with pity, he stretched out his hand, touched him, and said to him, 'I do will it. Be made clean.' The leprosy left him immediately…"

5) Jesus casts out the evil spirits…
"What have you to do with us, Son of God?"
~Matthew 8:28-33~

"When [Jesus] came to the other side, to the territory of the Gadarenes, two demoniacs who were coming from the tombs met him. They were so savage that no one could travel by that road. They cried out, 'What have you to do with us, Son of God? Have you come here to torment us before the appointed time?' Some distance away a herd of many swine was feeding. The demons pleaded with him, 'If you drive us out, send us into the herd of swine.' And he said to them, 'Go then!' They came out and entered the swine, and the whole herd rushed down the steep bank into the sea where they drowned. The swineherds ran away, and when they came to the town they reported everything, including what had happened to the demoniacs."

Mysteries of the Miracles Reflections

Jesus makes the lame man walk

A. It's all about gratitude, these Mysteries of the Miracles. We experience Jesus' healing and comfort—how He brings life to those in need. And all we can say is "Thank You."

How many of us have been, at one time or another, like the lame man—unable to walk our paths, unable to walk our *Christian* paths because our spirituality was "lame"? We didn't have the strength to lift ourselves above our pettiness, our helplessness, our sinfulness. It's as if we were stuck in the mud of our reluctance—even our ignorance—mulling over which leg to prop up first, or whether we would ever be able to stand on our own two feet again.

But Jesus meets us in our crippledness and lifts us up; He strengthens our ankles, heals our legs, and helps us to see how we can be a part of His Kingdom-building, His *promise* to the world. We are the ones who must bring the hand of God to the people of the world—blessed by the Holy Spirit and the loving touch of our Creator.

Have you allowed the Savior to *make you walk*, or do you lie helpless and hopeless in a world of broken dreams and restless sleep? Remember, Jesus' miracles are all about gratitude. We can see this in the response of the lame man, as he rejoiced in the Lord and spread the word of God's mercy, after being freed from his lameness. I believe that those who were healed by Christ were some of the most enthusiastic evangelizers. What do *you* think?

* * * * * * * * * * * *

B. A few years ago, I saw the most amazing thing. An African deacon, whom I had only seen in a wheelchair, with no legs, came walking down the aisle of a church—gingerly, slowly, arduously—but WALKING—on prosthetic legs. It was a joyous scene, as his daughter stood at the front of the church, encouraging his progress!

Who says miracles don't happen these days?

Jesus told the lame man, "Pick up your mat and go home." Do you have the courage to listen to the Master, pick up whatever mat you are lying on, and get up and move? What is stopping you?

* * * * * * * * * * * *

C. Today, while on my T.E.R.M. rosary walk, I realized that I spend an awful lot of time looking eight to ten feet in front of me, staring at the ground for bumps and holes in the pavement. I've been missing all of the scenery around me—for years. So I have begun to lift my eyes and notice what is happening around me.

Jesus observed all that was around Him, often spotting people in need, and observing nature and people; using the scenes from daily life, He created the many parables which He spoke about to the crowds.

Of the many healings brought about by Jesus, there is the one in which He made a blind man see. I believe the significance of this act goes far beyond the act itself.

What was going on inside the blind man's head when he had been cured? Did he desire to have a hand in helping the many people around him who were suffering? Now this man could play a part in bettering the lives of others because he could *see* them. He probably had greater compassion for people because of his own trials when he was blind and unable to see their struggles.

Yes, Jesus worked a great miracle when He made the blind man see, but it may have been a greater miracle by expanding the heart of this once-blind man to truly serve his fellow man through generous acts, now that he could "see."

Jesus feeds the 5,000

A. It's been said that feeding the five thousand was not a miracle of multiplicity but of transformation. More than once I've heard someone say that what really happened was that Jesus stirred generosity in the hearts of the five thousand so that those who had carried food with them (but kept it hidden, reluctant to share it) shared it with their neighbors. They say that when Jesus spoke, these people decided to take out what they had and divide it with those around them.

But this does not explain how they would have all carried the same lunch—bread and fish—or how all of them would have had the same bright idea at the same time. No, it WAS a true miracle—a miracle of creating something that wasn't there before.

Jesus had turned water into wine, walked on the water, made a lame man walk, and raised a child from the dead—why couldn't He feed a great number of people? We don't know how He did it, but, "With God, all things are possible."

God is so gracious that He knows how to serve a banquet for the masses. Scripture says that there were twelve baskets of scraps left over. It seems that God decided it's better to have too much food than too little. No one went away unsatisfied!

This is an important theme of Jesus' stories about His Father: the generosity and integrity of a God who will never abandon us and always take care of us. Who could ask for anything better?

* * * * * * * * * * * *

B.
> *"When the disciples were concerned that there was not enough food to feed the hungry crowds, Jesus took what they had and blessed it. Giving thanks for God's gifts, he multiplied them, and had more than enough to feed the crowds."*
>
> ~ *Daily Word*

The emphasis here is on giving thanks. Jesus gave thanks to His Father for all the blessings He had received, and for the blessings which all those around Him had received through Him. Jesus was not merely the cup of suffering but the blessing cup. From performing miracles, to preaching the Word, to welcoming the little children, the presence of Jesus was a blessing to whomever He met. Even when He challenged others, such as the Pharisees, He did so with a loving heart—no matter how harsh His words may have sounded.

Feeding the five thousand was much like the Last Supper, where He offered Himself to the world as a sacrificial lamb. God took the ordinary and made it incredible—amazing—empowering. God has a way of *making a way out of "no way,"* especially when we are least expecting it. Thank You, God, for Your powerful ways!

* * * * * * * * * * * *

C. Some "mega churches" hold five thousand occupants or more…and Jesus said, "You will do even greater things then I." Imagine "feeding the Word of God" to a vast crowd, or spreading the gift of the Holy Spirit to the masses—this is what technology allows us to do these days. Pope John Paul II once said Mass for 100,000 people. And Jesus says, "You will do even greater things then I." Can you believe it?

Jesus makes the blind man see

A. While cool water splashed over her hands from a pump, the letters W-A-T-E-R, being spelled out in her hands, finally had meaning. It was at that moment that Helen Keller broke out of the prison of darkness that had bound her ever since a profound illness had left her blind and deaf. Although she could still not *see* with her eyes or *hear* with her ears, she could understand, and curiosity was unleashed in her mind and heart. Her teacher, Anne Sullivan, became an agent of Christ at that moment, helping a blind girl to see.

Often in our lives, it is this very curiosity that helps us to "see." Curiosity may involve something as simple as stopping to inspect the intricacies of a flower in a nearby planter, or it might mean empathizing with a man who is struggling with a poor social habit such as constantly cutting people off in conversation. "Seeing" may involve keeping up to date on pertinent social issues, or observing when a son or daughter needs to be listened to. We SEE with our hearts, with our understanding, with non-judgmental attitudes.

Understanding is the baseline for SEEING. Jesus helped the blind man perceive much more than what his eyes could see—He enabled the man to see with his heart, so that he knew that Jesus was the Messiah, unlike most of those who witnessed the miracle. This man lived the miracle of seeing *and* of knowing!

Jesus' miracles were always bringing light to the body, mind, and spirit. He knew that conversion of body would help lead to conversion of heart. But do you and I need a miracle to SEE? Or can we be believers without dramatic miracles taking place in our bodies? Perhaps witnessing or hearing about a miracle will be enough for our own transformation.

* * * * * * * * * * * * *

B. The biblical words "walk by faith, not by sight," bring together the curing of the paralytic and the curing of the blind man in a unique way. We are called to walk, but not to depend on what we see. We must move beyond visible evidence and "see" with our hearts.

Faith means believing even when you are uncertain; seeing even when you do not see; and walking even though you cannot see the path that stretches out before you. The trick is to be in touch with the Lord in order to understand that you are being led. Faith rests on the belief that you have a God who loves you. Know that, if you fall, you will always be caught; or if you stumble, you will always be restored to stability, through His mercy.

There are so many kinds of blindness, but Jesus can cure them all. Will you let Him help you see?

Jesus cures the leper

A. In Mark 1:40–42, *"A leper came to [Jesus] [and kneeling down] begged him and said, 'If you wish, you can make me clean.' Moved with pity, he stretched out his hand, touched him, and said to him, 'I do will it. Be made clean.' The leprosy left him immediately, and he was made clean."*

But did you notice? The leper came to Jesus *knowing* that he could be healed. He knew Jesus could do it, if He wanted to. His belief, his faith, not only brought about his healing through Jesus, but also brought about healing qualities within himself. Do you think he would have been healed if he had gone up to Jesus with this attitude: "Well, I don't really believe in this healing stuff, but I guess I can take your word for it that maybe you can heal me?"

Perhaps Jesus would not have had the motivation to heal (although he could have by the sheer reality of who He was), but the man would not have been able to *receive*; he would not be receptive towards a healing touch, even if it was offered to him. Jesus spoke the truth when He told the woman after she was cured of hemorrhaging, "Your faith has saved you." She believed, she knew, and, indeed, she was healed!

The leper had faith that Jesus' compassion would reach out to him and heal his leprosy. You see, his belief made it possible; Jesus' grace made it happen!

* * * * * * * * * * * *

B. "Be made clean." These words of Jesus remind me of the words which Catholics profess just before receiving the Eucharist: "Lord, I am not worthy that You should enter under my roof, but only say the word and my soul shall be healed." These are words of humility due to our unworthiness, but they also testify to our belief that the Lord has the power to heal us.

Notice how the prayer says, "only say the word." Jesus touched the leper and said simply, "I do will it. Be made clean." He didn't perform a dramatic outward act. He didn't pray for ten or fifteen minutes, saying long, fancy words to His Father, as some preachers do. He just said, "Be made clean." These few words were enough.

I remember a time when I was suffering from depression and, during Mass, I couldn't wait until the point in the liturgy when we say: "But only say the word and my soul shall be healed." I believed then, as I do now, that there is something special about professing my belief that Jesus can heal me, that He can comfort me, that He can perform a great work.

It starts with *our* belief. God can do all things, but not if we don't let Him. It's more than just "positive attitude stuff." Faith is something deeper, as it was with the leper, who KNEW Jesus could heal him, and who knew that faith in Jesus' healing power would be the first step to his cure. So he took that leap: "If you wish, you can make me clean!" The first step to a cure is to believe that you CAN be healed. Second, you must be humble enough to let Him heal you. Finally, allow your belief, and His love, to make the healing a reality.

Jesus casts out the evil spirits

A. In Jesus' day, many things that were inexplicable in the human condition were often considered to be caused by the presence of a "demon" or an "unclean spirit." There was demonic possession, of course, but even physical and mental handicaps and diseases would have appeared to be the result of such possession.

So where do these evil spirits lurk in our day and age? Well, schizophrenia and bipolar disorder have been proven to be mental illnesses that can be managed by medications and therapy. Their symptoms don't spring from evil spirits but from chemical imbalances, and in some cases, from trauma. But there is evil in the world, no doubt of that. It is interesting that Jesus talks of "unclean spirits." They were real demons, but let's also remember that even without possession we may have "dirtiness of heart" that surrounds us when we find ourselves in sin.

Just look at a few of the seven deadly sins: lust, envy, and gluttony. Impurity of thought: this is lust. Lust is the entertaining of sexual desires that keep us away from Godly thoughts. Dirtiness of feelings: this happens when envy leads us astray, causing division between ourselves and others. And dirtiness of action: gluttony, in which we eat our way into happiness, favoring our palate over all else. Yes, we have unclean spirits these days, which cause murderous, adulterous, thieving acts—and result in much trouble and sorrow. Limiting our TV viewing, which often glorifies death by its endless portrayal of murder and mayhem, may be a good place to start in our pursuit of virtue. What demon do YOU need cast out? And when will you pray for this miracle?

* * * * * * * * * * * *

B. Jesus cast out the evil spirits, and imparted the presence of grace. If He had not, the void caused by the evil spirits' leaving would probably have soon been filled by even worse spirits.

Jesus was always being identified by the evil spirits as the Son of God. Why? How did they know? And how were the people unaware of this? The evil spirits knew who Jesus was and feared He would destroy them. All they cared about was survival. They just wanted to feed off of their hosts and drain them of power.

But Jesus came to save suffering souls from the misery of being possessed. So He was seen casting out demons in many instances in the Bible. He set people free from the bondage of evil spirits. Evil does not have a place in the Kingdom, and He saved people from its clutches. Unclean spirits are no match for the Holy Spirit.

Chapter 3
Prince of Peace Mysteries

Prayed on Saturdays

1. Blessed are the peacemakers
2. Peace! Be still!
3. Peaceful prayer in the deserted places
4. Peaceful patience
5. Peace be with you

Biblical Citations

1) "Blessed are the peacemakers…"— The Beatitudes
~Matthew 5:9~

"Blessed are the peacemakers, for they will be called children of God."

2) "Peace! Be still!" …Jesus calms the storm.
~Mark 4:35-41~

"On that day, when evening had come, [Jesus] said to them, 'Let us go across to the other side.' And leaving the crowd behind, they took him with them in the boat, just as he was. Other boats were with him. A great gale arose, and the waves beat into the boat, so that the boat was already being swamped. But he was in the stern, asleep on the cushion; and they woke him up and said to him, 'Teacher, do you not care that we are perishing?' He woke up and rebuked the wind, and said to the sea, 'Peace! Be still!' Then the wind ceased, and there was a dead calm. He said to them, 'Why are you afraid? Have you still no faith?' And they were filled with great awe and said to one another, 'Who then is this, that even the wind and sea obey him?'" (*New Revised Standard Version*)

3) Jesus' peaceful prayer in the deserted places.
~Luke 5:15-16~

"The report about [Jesus] spread all the more, and great crowds assembled to listen to him and to be cured of their ailments, but he would withdraw to deserted places to pray."

4) Jesus' peaceful patience in waiting for His time to come.
~John 16:31-33~

"Jesus answered them, 'Do you believe now? Behold, the hour is coming and has arrived when each of you will be scattered to his own home and you will leave me alone. But I am not alone, because the Father is with me. I have told you this so that you may have peace in me. In the world you will have trouble, but take courage, I have conquered the world.'"

5) "Peace be with you," Jesus says to the apostles when He appears behind locked doors.
~John 20:19-23~

"On the evening of that first day of the week, when the doors were locked, where the disciples were, for fear of the Jews, Jesus came and stood in their midst and said to them, 'Peace be with you.' When he had said this, he showed them his hands and his side. The disciples rejoiced when they saw the Lord. [Jesus] said to them again, 'Peace be with you. As the Father has sent me, so I send you.' And when he had said this, he breathed on them and said to them, 'Receive the holy Spirit. Whose sins you forgive are forgiven them, and whose sins you retain are retained.'"

PRINCE OF PEACE MYSTERIES REFLECTIONS

Blessed are the peacemakers

A. Jesus said, "Blessed are the peacemakers, for they will be called children of God." Wow! To be considered a child of God is a very high honor. I only know one Son of God, and He Himself is saying that the peacemakers will be like Him—they will be children of God! This must be true then, since He IS the Prince of Peace and the Lord of Lords, and He calls us to do what the Father wishes.

"Blessed are the peacemakers." Jesus, the Prince of Peace, is teaching us how important peace is. Peace is not merely the absence of war or conflict, but a calmness of heart and stillness of mind that changes the dull and drab into the glowing Presence of God. To be able to bring peace to a difficult situation is one of the most fulfilling experiences I have ever had. I feel blessed to have opportunities to be a peacemaker. To be considered a "child of God" outshines every other self-description I have ever had. For, as the gospel song proclaims, "Our God is an awesome God!"

* * * * * * * * * * * * *

B. It seems that the peacemakers are always the ones to attract hatred. Dr. Martin Luther King Jr. led peaceful protests in the 1950s and 1960s. These protests inadvertently brought out the cruelest, most hateful side of many people. National TV exposure was one of the main weapons of the Civil Rights Movement because it brought into people's living rooms the injustice and devastation of segregation, violence, and discrimination.

Peacemakers don't create violence. They unmask it. They allow it to come forth and rear its ugly head. Why do you think Jesus was singled out? Jesus was speaking the truth about the hypocrites and the deceivers. He unmasked evil in order to promote goodness, and to reveal the Will of His Father.

"Blessed are the peacemakers." Jesus was the foremost peacemaker.

Peace! Be still!

A. Imagine this story in your own life: a crisis arises. You feel fear and weakness, you are trapped. And there is Jesus, right in front of you, saying "Peace! Be still!" It may have seemed as though He was sleeping in the back of the boat, but "our God is an on-time God," as the old gospel song goes. It's God's timing, God's way, that we need to trust—even when the storm is raging, even when we feel we have little hope left.

It is so easy to say, but so difficult to live out.

* * * * * * * * * * * * *

B. Imagination can become a great friend. With this particular mystery, I imagine I am one of the disciples in that sinking boat. My security, my peace of mind, my hope, is threatened by a negative event or an on-going aggravation. And I realize I have my Savior there, but He is sleeping in the back of the boat. So I rush and wake Him. I exclaim, "Can't you see we are all perishing!" and He gets up and heads to the bow of the boat. There, He stretches out His arms and rebukes the wind: "Peace! Be still!"

In my imagination, He stills the rushing waters of my mind; He quiets the raging wind of my unwieldy visualizations; He stands tall before me as the seas of my heart become calm; my pulse stops racing. The image of cool, still waters sets my mind free, and I can think clearly again.

This is one way to experience a simple spiritual awakening. Give your willingness over to your imagination and see where the Holy Spirit will take you.

Peace in the deserted places

A. Just as He often sought quiet, deserted places to pray, Jesus meets us in our deserted places. Jesus sought out people who were lost in some way or another: lost in hunger (mental, physical, or spiritual), lost in sin, lost in darkness, lost in immobility, lost in pride, lost in destructive habits. So, too, Jesus meets us in our "lostness." And He wants to help us find a home.

The songwriter Joe Jackson sang, "You can't get what you want 'til you know what you want." This sounds too simple, too obvious, but how many of us are searching for happiness, although we have never defined what that happiness might be? We run around and around, chasing our tails, trying to find who we really are and what we really want.

Jesus wants to stop the foolishness of our endless flight from ourselves, and ground us in His wisdom. This wisdom sounds so childlike and simple:

> You are loved
> You are capable
> You are ready

We must be ready to serve Him, no matter how incapable and insignificant we may feel. It is the will of God that we move out of ourselves and extend our time and talents by loving others. In all we do, we are to love—love God, and love others. These, says Jesus, are the two greatest commandments.

Is there anything blocking you from this calling? If so, you may need to take a little time to discover where Jesus knows you are "lost." He has prepared a home for you, inside your heart, if you'll only seek Him there.

* * * * * * * * * * * *

B. Moments of intimate prayer with God are so special. I find this quiet time and solitude on my T.E.R.M. rosary walks. Praying my T.E.R.M. rosary *and* getting a good walk in at the same time is a perfect combination for me. How do you find yourself best able to pray?

In deserted places, as Jesus modeled for us, we can find guidance and PEACE which we may not encounter at any other time. I hope you seek out your deserted places in order to commune with God. It is a beautiful thing!

Jesus' peaceful patience

A. Jesus knew, coming into Jerusalem, that the end of His life was drawing near. He had predicted and pronounced His death many times to the apostles, although none of them "got it" (or wanted to *get it*). How could He travel down that road into the city of His doom with such confidence? Scripture wrote about Jesus' concerns that others would attempt to make Him an earthly king. He managed to quickly get away from them. He seemed to have a "peaceful patience" about letting these instances be resolved, in time. He had patience with the process.

Also, since He knew He was going to die a horrible, painful death, it seems possible that, in His Godly-humanness, He had some apprehension. He may have even had some fear about the outcome. After all, scripture says that Jesus was like us in all things but sin. So, fear of being tortured? I can see that Jesus being fearful may have been a possibility.

But He steadied Himself with *peaceful patience*, and lived in the moment, knowing full well what He would encounter. He is a great example for us when we face trials, that we can steady ourselves with the *peaceful patience* of Jesus. We can know that He is there for us, in all we do.

* * * * * * * * * * * *

B. Since Jesus was both God *and* man, he had feelings. And guess what? He experienced anxiety! Yes, He *knew*; He knew all that was going to happen to Him: the pain, the blood, the cuts and bruises.

   He knew the outcome too — He knew the end of the story. Jesus knew that He would die, and rise again. It's right there in the scriptures. Think about it: when you know for certain that you will end up in a good place, even hell-on-earth experiences are approachable, possible, conquerable.

   So WE are promised Eternal Life if we do His will. Are we any less certain as to what *our* outcome will be, as we struggle with our daily trials? Why are we not confident, as Jesus was? Do we REALLY believe, or are we half-hearted Christians who "talk the talk," but can't believe?

   This is the tallest order I can think of: *to live every day of our lives in preparation for eternity, as if we already possessed it!* Is this just wishful thinking? Well, if Jesus is Savior, He must be "saving" us *for* something! And He is saving us for the highest honor: to be children of God, and to receive the inheritance won by Jesus' total self-sacrifice. He has already won the battle. Why don't we receive the treasures, here and now?

* * * * * * * * * * * *

C. We have all experienced anxiety. But how do we deal with it? "I've got something on my mind." Have you ever said that? Five years ago, I had something on my mind. I had joined the cast of a mental-health-advocacy play called *Pieces* that required memorizing a two-page script. I had never done anything like that before, and it was an excruciating process for me.

First, I had to get over the word "practice" because it brought back vivid memories of my piano-lesson days in junior high, where I would pretend to practice, while not putting my full effort or heart into it because I really didn't want to play piano. So to "practice" my *Pieces* monologue was nearly impossible, at first.

Then I decided to tape record it so I could listen to myself recite it. But this meant I had to get it down on tape perfectly, so that I could listen to the real deal. That took about a week or two. Then it was time for listening, reading, and reciting—all the time with the thought in the back of my mind, "What if I go up there and blow it? Lose my place? Stall?" The anxiety was palpable.

The ever-present tension I experienced in those early days of learning a part cause me to wonder how Jesus must have felt, knowing He was going to give up His life, and so soon. I admire Him for His *peaceful patience*. It gives me hope that, when I have worries, I can rely on Him and the thought that "this is not the end of the world," which allows me to get back on task.

I am also reminded that "It's not all about me," and when I acknowledge this, I can relax in the realization that I *have* a Savior, and He has already *saved*. I have learned how to have faith in my abilities to pick up new things and run with them, whether it be a new script or a new job. What is on my mind can be in my heart—and can soon be in my repertoire. With peaceful patience, any mountain can be conquered.

Peace be with you

A. They are waiting behind locked doors, and Jesus appears before them. The apostles and His other followers are startled by the holy intrusion. They had been living in fear—fear of the Jews. But Jesus comes before them to reassure them that, indeed, He is risen.

Don't we all need reassurance at times? It's a basic human need. Jesus has compassion for this, and comes before His faithful ones in His risen flesh.

Yes, we must trust Jesus—He *won't* leave us alone! He is always with us, no matter how we try to lock Him out! He is with us in our pain, in our doubt, in our disbelief, and in our loneliness. He walks through the doors of our fears to comfort us, to confront us, to guide us, and to admonish us. He came for the broken and the disheartened—for that is who He came to save.

* * * * * * * * * * * *

B. I wrote this poem after reading John 20:19-23; these words inspired me to look inside myself for ways in which I had been holding others captive with lack of forgiveness.

...SHALL BE RETAINED

After Jesus appears behind locked doors, He says:
*"Whose sins you forgive are forgiven them,
and whose sins you retain are retained."*
(John 20:23)

Then I suddenly saw myself in the mirror
resentments, jealousies, self-hatreds galore
all the ugliness of my soul came pouring out
a spigot turned on full and water had begun spilling
onto the floor.

"Now I see where my anger was coming from!"
The answer had been revealed in one word…

"Retained."

So often I have held onto my resentments
as if hugging a snuggly teddy bear
grasping hold, never to give them up
for the strange comfort they provided me there.

Retained.

The petty jealousies I've embroiled in my fear-laden heart
like a flaming burger on a summertime grill
bursting with the juices of regret and lost pride
for my not having climbed a similar hill.

Retained.

I have felt "less-than" at times,
when comparing myself to a relative, colleague, or friend;
broken hearted and demeaned by crushing comparison
not knowing if my heart would ever mend.

Retained.

And the menacing self-pity entrenched in my psyche
that has smoldered for so many years isn't working
in the back of my sullen smoke-house mind
that's provided me with its savored meat of *grief lurking*.

Retained.

I know and see the ruins that my retention has created
and God now calls to my humbled heart born anew,
to turn "retained" into a healthy "letting go"
and find new ways of allowing love to flow from me to you.

Section II

Reflections for the Traditional Mysteries

(Joyful, Luminous, Sorrowful, and Glorious)

Chapter 4
The Joyful Mysteries

Monday—The Joyful Mysteries
The Annunciation, The Visitation,
The Nativity, The Presentation,
The Finding of Jesus in the Temple

The Annunciation

A. We know that an angel, Gabriel, appeared to Mary to inform her that she had been chosen to give birth to the Son of God. But when did conception occur?

My belief is that it took place at the exact moment when Mary said "Yes" to God. Why? Because God honored Mary's free will. He proposed to her, and she consented.

Think about this: as soon as Mary was asked to be Jesus' mother, she pronounced, "I am the handmaid of the Lord," and instantly, she had the beginnings of our Lord inside her, through the overshadowing of the Holy Spirit. Jesus, the Son of God, was developing within her. She believed in Jesus Christ. Therefore, by definition, Mary was the first Christian. Ponder this!

* * * * * * * * * * * * *

B. When she said "YES" to God's invitation to bear the Son of God, Mary's joy was expressed in her Magnificat, in Luke 1:46–50:

"My soul proclaims the greatness of the Lord; my spirit rejoices in God, my savior. For he has looked upon his handmaid's lowliness; behold, from now on will all ages call me blessed. The Mighty One has done great things for me, and holy is his name.

His mercy is from age to age to those who fear him…"

There was the promise of eternal joy *and* devastating pain—she would see her son become known as a great healer and preacher, then see Him tortured in the streets of Jerusalem; she would stand before His cross on Calvary, during His Passion. But she accepted all of this, knowing this would be her destiny, and placing all her trust in God.

* * * * * * * * * * * * *

C. Mary is chosen before her birth to be the mother of Jesus. She is the Immaculate Conception, conceived without sin. This being true, how can we view our lives as having a significant mission? How will God show us what we are destined to do, or who we are destined to be?

It really flies in the face of my staunch declaration that "predestination" is an impossibility, since God gave us all free will. But my strong belief does not take into account that a "mission" can be completed in a myriad of ways. The man who refused to go into the fields, in the biblical parable, changed his mind and indeed went to work. And the one who immediately agreed to work ended up not doing so.

I don't yet understand it, but maybe there is something to God having an ultimate destiny for all of us. We may have free will, but with God's guidance, we eventually find ourselves living out His Will. This reminds me of the 1994 film *Forrest Gump* where Forrest, a developmentally-challenged man, moves from adventure to adventure simply by living in the moment and reaching out with courage and integrity. He found his mission every step of the way from college football star to war hero, to long-distance runner, to millionaire, to loving father.

Forrest saw it this way:

```
   " . . . I don't know if Mama was right
or if it's . . . if it's Lieutenant Dan . . .
 I don't know if we each have a . . . destiny;
    or if we're all just floatin' around
         accidental-like, on a breeze . . .
                but, I think,
   I think it's BOTH----maybe both happening
             at the same time . . ."
                          (From the film's script)
```

This way of thinking truly appeals to me because it takes into consideration God's Will and man's effort. Like Forrest, I believe we have to help shape our own destiny—we have to put forth a courageous effort. Yet it is God's guidance and love which provide the motivation that greases the gears of this complex machine we call life. Mary needed to say YES to the Holy Spirit for Jesus to become incarnate within her. If she had chosen otherwise, we might have a very different world than we do now. Mary, in fear, could have put God off for a time, only choosing submission at a later date. Jesus might still have been born, but at a later date.

The odd and mysterious thing is that our intermittent indecision and even our tragedies may have been a part of the plan all along. The very things we consider thorns in our sides may be necessary for the Kingdom to come. So I pray, as Jesus did, that God's will be done, not mine. And I pray that I have the courage and stamina to follow through.

* * * * * * * * * * * *

D. Once, while praying on one of my walks, I was pondering what Our Lady of Guadalupe might mean, and to me, it means "one who holds HOPE." At the time of this apparition, AD 1531, Mary appeared to Juan Diego as an expectant mother, carrying our Lord in her womb. In the unborn Jesus, we have a Redeemer who has not yet been born, whose mission is imminent but has not yet formally begun. And Mary speaks to Juan Diego, the man who saw the apparition, as a mother. Mary is about to bring the *light of the world* into the world. She is the glimmer of light in a broken, oblivious world. She *held HOPE* within her womb.

The Visitation

A. Who was visiting whom? It wasn't just Mary visiting her cousin Elizabeth, but Jesus visiting His cousin John: "When Elizabeth heard Mary's greeting, the infant leaped in her womb, and Elizabeth, filled with the holy Spirit, cried out in a loud voice and said, 'Most blessed are you among women, and blessed is the fruit of your womb.'" (Luke 1:41–42) This is where the "Hail Mary" prayer comes from!

How can those in the womb "visit" one another? The Holy Spirit can do amazing things! The question is, "Does destiny come with conception?" Is what we are meant to do in our lives built into us? The world would have us believe that whatever happens, happens. Not for Jesus and John, and not with eyes of faith. John was destined to introduce Jesus to the world, just as he did when he first "met" Him that day when he leaped with joy in Elizabeth's womb, even before their births.

And where does this leave us? Are we destined to do good, to succeed, or to do anything at all? My belief is that we are guided in a certain direction. We might lose our way, and need to be corrected or re-corrected, and guided again. We are given glimpses of our true selves, but often lose the vision in the fog of the complexities of daily living.

When has someone given you an introduction to yourself? Have you been *visited* by the Holy Spirit through the words and deeds of others, or in ways that have given you an image of who you are and who you will become? Sometimes this can happen on a retreat, or in church, or while out on a walk, or even during a scholastic seminar. But somehow, somewhere, God is reaching out to us, seeking to show us The Way.

At one time, this kind of awakening came in the form of my wife's contribution to a speech for a seminar which I'd been working on for eighteen months. It was an ethics philosophy that I call "The Corsair Code," in which I outline three aims for pursuing interpersonal excellence. These aims are: 1) showing sincere respect; 2) living a life of integrity; and 3) expressing authenticity. I am certain that the Holy Spirit came upon my wife and I to enable us to create the final version of this speech in one hour of brainstorming—something I could have never done alone. Sandra introduced *me* to *me* by assisting in the creation of a meaningful project.

What does this have to do with destiny? Well, twenty-five years ago I was part of a seminar that discussed many of these principles and I made a silent vow at that time that, one day, I would give back what I had been given. And now, with "The Corsair Code" well on its way, it is nearing the time for me to give back. I don't know if I was "destined" to change lives through this seminar—or if I ever will. But I *do* know that I'm being led by the Spirit, and isn't that what's most important?

* * * * * * * * * * * *

B. The first evangelization of Jesus Christ took place between two women: Mary and her cousin Elizabeth. They rejoiced in the wonder and glory of the angel Gabriel's appearance and on the part Mary was to play in the prophesied events of the Messiah's coming. And John the Baptist took his cue at that moment, he who would later be the man who would usher in the ministry of Jesus. Many of the "followers of Jesus" were women and they got little or no credit for all they did for Him. And with the modern-day human leadership, oftentimes, women are not listed to or respected for their expertise…either nun or lay person. Don't women need to be given more credit in the Church for all they have done, and all the goodness they have bestowed on us all with their extraordinary influence? Mary and Elizabeth show us examples of deep faith and belief in God's goodness.

The Nativity

A. The joy of Jesus' birth can be overwhelming at times. Our amazement over the fact that God came down to earth in human form, to be one of us, is incredible, and, yes, overwhelming. In Luke 5:7, we see how Simon Peter experienced the superabundance of God's generosity when Jesus commanded him to throw his nets over the side of the boat after a disappointing evening on the lake. When Peter complied, his nets nearly burst with fish and the boats almost sank with the load!

This reminds me of a quote by the writer Marianne Williamson:

"Our deepest fear is not that we are inadequate. Our deepest fear is that we are powerful beyond measure. It is our light, not our darkness, that most frightens us."

This is my reflection upon reading the above quote:

Our Greatest Fear

Our greatest fear is lying in here (placing hand over heart)
*it's an aching like no other
that the gift of our BEST SELF
may be locked inside.*

*A fear that—if we see it
in here* (heart)
and know it in here (head)—
we'll be called to express it out there.

*What we need is a way—
a way to pull off the blinders
and truly SEE.
See ourselves for who we really are
see that our potential is NOT our prison
and our possibilities are not our plague.*

*We need to find out who we are!
Find out what is possible!
Find out new ways to make it happen!*

*Our greatest fear can be the spring of our deepest joy
as we take on that fear like a mountain to be conquered
and climb the frosty peaks of discouragement and pain
to discover the heights of belief:
belief in self
belief in others
belief in the positive possibilities
that spring from the depths of joy.*

*And the change can happen
the change WILL happen
every time we believe in ourselves
and replace the fear of potential greatness
with the joy of knowing our greatness.*

*The change WILL happen
it will surprise you
and make you come alive!*

* * * * * * * * * * * *

B. Christmas is supposed to be the happiest time of year. It's usually happiest, I guess, for the merchants who take advantage of shopping sprees and the obligation that most people feel to give Christmas gifts. The joy over the birth of our Lord has been desecrated by rampant commercialism and the over-emphasis on gift-giving. What would the celebration of Jesus' birth be like without all this?

What if it were like the ending scene of the film *How the Grinch Stole Christmas,* when the Whos found that their Christmas preparations had been stolen, and they stood holding hands in the snow, rejoicing anyway? This Dr. Seuss story, which I loved as a child, means so much more to me now. I pray that I can celebrate Christmas in more profound ways, and share my love through simple, thoughtful actions. That is my goal this Christmas.

The Presentation

A. How happy Mary and Joseph must have been to bring the Christ Child into the temple! Mary knew that she was bringing the Son of God into this place of worship, and it would be Joseph who would teach the Child Jesus the Scriptures, the Word of God, since he was the head of the Holy Family. Jesus was presented to the world and given His name at a crucial moment in history.

With Mary and Joseph's guidance, the wonderful qualities of Jesus emerged, as He grew. The presentation was just the beginning of that glorious journey.

* * * * * * * * * * * *

B. How could Mary hold back the news about this baby, that He was the Son of God? Perhaps she was filled with anticipation, eager to share the Good News that her son was the "one who is to come." Can you imagine trying to keep a secret like that from those around you? It must have been pleasantly excruciating! What must it have meant to others when they named the Child "Jesus," which means "God saves"? Would Mary and Joseph have been seen as arrogant for giving Him such a name?

I think Mary was so humble of heart that she was able to quell the temptation to announce to others or call out God's praises for blessing her as the mother of the Son of God, a supreme honor. She knew that God had great plans for her,

her husband, and her son, and no proclamation could match the inner gratitude that she showed God in the quietness of her heart. She was truly blessed!

Jesus is found safe in the Temple

A. It's hard to fathom the depths of relief which Mary and Joseph must have felt when they found Jesus in the temple. The agony of His loss was replaced by the shock of this blessing: the Boy found after days of searching everywhere. Perhaps they had gone to the temple to offer sacrifices to God in hopes of finding Jesus.

Being found is one of the most beautiful experiences in the world, not only for the person found, but for the finder. Jesus seemed surprised that His parents wouldn't know where He was. Mary and Joseph probably experienced the relief-followed-by-distress response: "Oh, thank God you are safe, but how could you do this to us?" Then a heavy, long hug. Being found is a strange and wonderful experience!

* * * * * * * * * * * *

B. Mary and Joseph had some responsibility in this, too. They assumed that Jesus was with relatives in the caravan that headed back to Nazareth. They weren't sure where He was and must have assumed He was safe, perhaps due to what others told them. So when He came up missing, some of their emotions must have been guilt and remorse that they had not been better stewards of their Son's welfare.

* * * * * * * * * * * *

C. Who was really lost? Jesus, or Mary and Joseph? Yes, Jesus had been lost by them. He could not be found. But He was in His Father's house—the Temple. His mother and foster-father were the lost ones: lost in fear and grief and guilt and worry. So Jesus was not the only one found safe in the Temple.

Have you ever felt lost? Have you ever "lost yourself"? It is a horrible place to be. This has happened to me many times, mostly due to my bipolar disorder—the pit of depression and the out-of-control mania. Lost, feeling dead, feeling "too alive," trying to find balance and peace.

I can relate to the scene of Jesus being lost. What is your experience? And if you feel lost right now, you can be found in the heart of Jesus, our Savior.

Chapter 5

The Luminous Mysteries

Thursday—The Luminous Mysteries

The Baptism of the Lord, The Wedding Feast at Cana, The Proclamation of the Kingdom, The Transfiguration, The Institution of the Eucharist

The Baptism of the Lord

A. Isn't baptism meant to wash us clean of original sin—the sin of Adam and Eve? If so, why was Jesus baptized at all? Not only was He sinless, but His mother was born without original sin. Was He baptized out of pure ritual?

There was a very good reason why He was baptized. It was an outward sign from His father that HE would become the channel of ultimate forgiveness, to cleanse all people through the glory of His life, death, and Resurrection. "At his baptism, 'the heavens were opened'—the heavens that Adam's sin had closed—and the waters were sanctified by the descent of Jesus and the Spirit, a prelude to the creation" (*Catechism of the Catholic Church*, 536). Jesus brought holiness to the waters of His baptism.

* * * * * * * * * * * *

B. Jesus received the most beautiful affirmation from His Father: "And a voice came from heaven, 'You are my beloved son; with you I am well pleased.'" (Luke 3:22) Imagine how Jesus felt upon hearing these words. What joy! What love for His Father!

Have you ever experienced a Godly affirmation in your life? A fellow parishioner of mine said that she has felt this many times while serving in a literacy program for adults. She believes that God has touched her with this ministry not only to serve others but to affirm her in her personal life as a Christian woman.

Another woman at church has felt this holy affirmation in her work as a certified nursing assistant, serving the elderly who are in need. She considers it a blessing to serve in this way, although it is back-breaking work. She experiences a lot of satisfaction when she is complimented on a job well done. God affirms her through this strenuous labor.

* * * * * * * * * * * *

C. Baptism: Jesus had no sin to be taken away. He was soon to be going into the desert for forty days, at the end of which He would be tempted by the devil; Jesus Himself would experience the ways in which we ourselves are tempted. He had been affirmed by His father, cooled by the waters, and sent forth to the testing grounds of solitude. Could there be any better way to begin His ministry?

The Wedding Feast at Cana (Jesus turns water into wine)

A. Jesus' first public miracle was made at the request of His mother who said, "Do whatever he tells you," to the servants. (John 2:5) He then turns four casks of water into the best wine ever tasted.

Is it so impossible that, just as Jesus turned the water into wine, He could have likewise turned wine into His blood, as witnessed at the Last Supper? Rather, this seems like a natural progression—the disappointment of running out of wine at a huge wedding (whereupon more wine was produced than anyone could drink)—and then the solemnity of the Passover celebration with His friends, where He turned the bread and wine into His body and blood—all of this ultimately leading to His Resurrection.

In His miracles, Jesus was always giving others exactly what they needed, right at their moment of need. From curing the leper, to giving the blind man sight, to raising Lazarus, to creating wine out of water; He was giving drink to the thirsty, clothing to the naked, food to the hungry. And this is what He asks us to do, for in one place in the gospels He says something to the effect of, "You will do even greater things than I."

We have been called to serve, as Jesus served, but in our own ways, with our own gifts. We may not turn water into wine, but isn't saving a life through CPR, comforting one who is in depression, or being a pilot who saves passengers and crew from a fatal crash much more "miraculous" than turning water into wine? We have heroes all around us, and miracles happen every day. And God is the source of these great happenings! Praise Him!

* * * * * * * * * * * *

B. "His mother said to the servers, 'Do whatever He tells you.'" (John 2:5) Mary seemed to feel that it was time for her son to go public with His powers as the Son of God. I imagine that she was very proud of Jesus, rather like the day He took His first step as a child. Turning water into wine *WAS* His first step in revealing His divinity.

Without Mary's nudge, without her faith *in Him,* He may have gone much farther down the road before performing His first miracle. *A mother's touch* made all the difference. Mary had an advantage. She knew at the outset, when Gabriel came to her and proclaimed that she would give birth to the Son of God, that her son was, indeed, special—that He was the Messiah. Somehow she knew when it was the right time for Him to come out of His previous world and into the new. What a blessing!

She probably also knew that He had to start small and work His way up. If she had prompted Him to raise a dead man or make a blind man see, it may have been possibly too shocking for witnesses. Mary knew her son. She loved Him, and knew when to push.

* * * * * * * * * * * *

C. Once, while meditating on the mystery of the Wedding Feast at Cana, I began to think of how a modern-day celebration would be nearly halted by running out of wine, as it happened the night Jesus turned the water into wine. Or what if the guests at this contemporary party ran out of enthusiasm? What transformation could Jesus perform that would bring a celebration "back to life"?

Then I thought of a certain person in my life with whom I am somewhat estranged. I imagined a warming—like wine going down my throat—between me and that person, and how Jesus could "lubricate" our relationship through love.

Suddenly, there I was—in my mind, hugging her—this person I thought I would never hug—with softness and true humility. Jesus had turned water into wine in my heart, and I now know that when I see her again, the Love of Christ will flow over the previously jagged rocks of our relationship, and sooth the burning thirst for closeness that I want with all people, in my venture to become the caring man I want to be, and am becoming.

The Proclamation of the Kingdom

A. In the gospels, it says that when Jesus first read publicly from the book of Isaiah, He ended by stating that this prophecy had come to pass in their hearing that day. All were mesmerized by this proclamation, and by His Presence. But when He went on to say that many Gentiles had greater faith than they did, they became so enraged that they brought Him to the edge of a cliff and attempted to throw Him off.

What an entry into the life He was called to lead! What did Jesus think of their reaction? I believe that He was well aware of the possible violent response, because He knew the penalty for blasphemy—it was very harsh. And to many of His people, His claims to have divine authority would appear to be blasphemy, since they did not know that He was God.

What a chance He was taking! And why was He not flung off the cliff to His death? Because He knew it was *not His time* yet, and maybe, somehow, the persecutors knew it too. He was only at the beginning stage of proclaiming the Word, and the crowd must have wised up. Think about it. This may just have been one of Jesus' first miracles: to placate an angry crowd that was about to kill Him; to calm them enough so that He could walk through them to safety.

* * * * * * * * * * * *

B. What was it like for Jesus to speak those first words in public? He had discussed the Torah with the learned men in the temple at age twelve, when He had stayed behind after the departure of His family's caravan to be in His Father's house; but THIS—this was different.

Jesus was to read words from the prophet Isaiah about the coming Kingdom of God. I was reflecting on this while on my T.E.R.M. rosary walk one day: Jesus' first public words—what could they have been? Then it came to me. Perhaps He spoke of just that: His Father's Kingdom, and the goodness that comes to those who follow in God's way.

Then I thought about how maybe, just maybe, MY mission is to do the same. Perhaps all my efforts to lecture on respect and personal growth topics actually shrink in importance when compared to the light of God's Word. Maybe I have a primary responsibility to teach the Word of God, and to share with others Jesus' love for us.

Recently I volunteered to be an RCIA (Right of Christian Initiation for Adults) teacher—to teach the Catholic faith to those hoping to become Catholic. Sometimes God works right around and within us and we never realize it. I will be giving up Tuesday evenings to be an RCIA instructor, but maybe this *is* my calling—to bring knowledge and encouragement to those seeking to know Jesus more fully.

All this inspiration to truly live out my faith came from a simple time of prayer, meditating on the mysteries of the life of Christ. I believe that Mother Mary, perhaps in a special way through her title as Our Lady of Guadalupe, is multi-blessing me and those I pray for during my T.E.R.M. rosary walks. I encourage you to pray the T.E.R.M. rosary. With the additional fifteen mysteries, it is a wondrous "bouquet of prayer" that I imagine Our Lady welcomes very graciously. Since I began praying it on August 16th, 2008, I have been a part of a miraculous transformation. Mary has shown me the life of Jesus each day, and I am forever blessed from these encounters with our Lord!

The Transfiguration

A. This mystery has always baffled me. Why did Jesus decide to show His glory to Peter, James, and John? What was the significance? He had showed them His mighty deeds numerous times, so what was the purpose of showing them His heavenly glory?

Maybe someone on earth had to glimpse His divine glory before His Passion took place. Someone had to know for sure that He was not of this world, that He had come from a place of ultimate eminence. And they (Peter, James, and John) were chosen to be those witnesses. It seems strange that they would fall away from Him at His time of need during His Passion, especially after this vision of glory. It just goes to show how quickly we can forget even the most amazing things in our lives. What in your life do you need to remember?

* * * * * * * * * * * *

B. I belong to a Catholic gospel choir and sing in the bass section. I used to be a tenor, but was switched because we had twelve tenors and only two basses. The basses need numbers, not necessarily talent. The thing is, my vocal range is in between the two—I can't sing the higher tenor notes, nor the lower base notes. So I don't really fit in either section. But I try my best. Recently, before heading to go cross-country skiing, I prayed for the grace to see this gospel choir, and my challenges in it, in a new way.

While praying the Transfiguration mystery on the ski trail, God brought me to that new place. I was imagining Moses and Elijah standing by Jesus, in blazing white, while I gazed at the white snow before me as I skied along. I wondered how Peter, James, and John could have recognized Moses and Elijah, since they had never met them. I imagined Moses holding two large stone tablets and Elijah holding a large book—the Old Testament. Then, out of the blue, I came to realize that my choir practices were actually *prayer meetings*. As though I had seen Jesus myself in flashy whiteness, I saw the light: I was there to *praise God* at choir practice, and not to think of them as practices, or to be consumed by which notes I could or couldn't hit. I was awakened to see it as worship-time.

It can be funny how God inspires us at the oddest times—while skiing, for example! And yet I was transfigured in heart and mind. Choir became a multi-blessing, in the blink of an eye!

The Eucharist

A. Bread, wine, plates, cups, table, a gathering…such simple, such common, such wonderful components of a meal. We experience similar essentials every day. What made THIS event so special? Our Lord was celebrating the important Jewish feast of Passover with his disciples.

The Last Supper was Jesus' final earthly meal with His apostles. But only Jesus knew that this was His last meal with them! He was well aware of the sacrifice He was about to make.

To me, breaking the bread represented His sharing His life with all around Him: His words, His deeds, His compassion and kindness; His refusal to let evil go unchecked. The bread of (His) life that had come down from heaven was about to be broken in a new way—in His death.

This "cup of blessing" was the cup of His blood which would be spilled in just a few hours. He was to be tortured and crucified—the cruelest of punishments in His day. And crucified for what? For speaking the truth, for laying hands on lepers, for feeding the hungry, for making the blind see, for raising the dead—and for challenging the Pharisees. His crime was bringing life to Life!

It seems odd and amazing that, facing His death, He could raise a cup of wine without shaking so much that He spilled it; or how His voice didn't crack in fear so that He could barely give the blessing. The Eucharist is not merely about thanksgiving, but about courage—the courage to face great suffering with serenity, and to keep your faith.

* * * * * * * * * * * *

B. While walking and praying the Luminous Mysteries one night, I had this thought: at the wedding at Cana, Jesus performed the first "transubstantiation." He turned water into wine. A few seconds later, I had the most peculiar thought—a thought that made me feel like a dummy and a genius at the same time:

> "Hey! Jesus didn't save his first *transubstantiation*
> for the first priest who raised the bread and wine...
> this occurred at the moment Jesus gave thanks
> and said 'This is My body...this is My blood'!"

How could I have not seen this all these years? That means that the apostles were the first to eat and drink the body and blood of Christ, the night of the Last Supper. Why did Jesus do this? What was the purpose?

I'm wondering if it was because they were to be the first evangelizers of the New Covenant, the bringers of the Word, the first to receive the Holy Spirit in a new way at Pentecost. THIS, the first Eucharist, WAS receiving the Holy Spirit in a new and wonderful way—and an ever-present sign of Jesus' power to overcome all odds, by His Resurrection, and in our lives today.

We are truly strengthened for the journey due to the power of the Eucharist—given not merely as a *sign* of God's love, but the *reality* of His presence. What a blessing to be offered this eternal gift! It makes me feel honored to be a Catholic, and to believe in the transubstantiation as a Reality in my life.

* * * * * * * * * * * *

C. One Thanksgiving Day, my wife and I decided to serve at a meal program in urban Milwaukee. With over thirty volunteers, the program director made it clear that the most important duty of the day for many of us would be to simply interact with the guests and eat the meal with them. Although it was not what we had in mind when we decided to invest part of our Thanksgiving Day serving the poor, we became guests ourselves.

My wife and I sat with two homeless men, Don and Mark, who told us about their lives, discussed the strategies of the Green Bay Packers, and chatted about the cold weather soon to hit Milwaukee. It was delightful to speak with them and eat with them! I felt as though it were a Eucharistic moment, the sharing of Christ, in the midst of these troubled economic times.

What a blessing to be eating our turkey and stuffing with these middle-aged men who showed great gratitude for the meal provided, and who gave us pleasant conversation as well. Sandra and I thank God for being given the opportunity to share our strength and hope with them, and to have hopefully brightened that gloomy November afternoon.

* * * * * * * * * * * *

D. Recently, I was searching for a cure to my winter "blahs": the negative thoughts and feelings that have been plaguing me lately. I couldn't seem to get away from these transfixing attitudes. Then it occurred to me that I hadn't been thanking God for the simple, but important things in my life—a great meal, a smile from my wife, my health, and so on. Well, these are BIG things! It struck me that gratitude was and is missing from my life: the very essence of the Eucharist, which when translated means "thanksgiving." So I have re-included it in my winter diet and found happiness sitting there, at my table, like a welcome guest.

* * * * * * * * * * * *

E. Jesus offered His life to us when He said, "This is my body, which will be given up for you." The Bread of Life *is* His life—His teaching, preaching, healing, loving, touching. He brings us all together as His Body, then offers His Blood as He raises the cup, saying, "Do this in memory of me." His blood represents His death and the Salvation that He brought when He hung His head and died on the cross, only to rise on the third day.

Life and death lead to rising to new life—not only for Himself, but for us all. It is the ultimate blessing, the magnificent gesture of thanksgiving, represented so poignantly in the Eucharist, as Jesus offers His true body and blood, in the form of bread and wine. Think of it! The True Presence of Jesus Christ, given to us. God is amazing! Wouldn't you agree?

* * * * * * * * * * * * *

F. As He raised the bread, Jesus lifted up His body, His life—up on the cross—and the blood of Salvation came pouring down, to cleanse our weary, sinful souls.

Chapter 6
The Sorrowful Mysteries

Friday—Sorrowful Mysteries
The Agony in the Garden, The Scourging at the Pillar, The Crowning with Thorns, The Carrying of the Cross, The Crucifixion

The Agony in the Garden

A. It was not merely the agony of His approaching death that caused Him such anguish in the garden. It was also the agony of knowing that multitudes of people in the past, present, and future would reject His self-sacrifice and thus reject their own salvation. Jesus also understands those who suffer abuse and torture, similar to what He was about to endure. This is where we actually receive the empathetic suffering of Christ; the reality that Jesus *is* suffering WITH us—in time, at this very moment! At the moment of His Passion, He suffered in union with us, united with us each moment in time when we have suffered, are suffering, or will suffer.

Could this be? How could Jesus be suffering with us? "I will be with you always," is a promise made by Jesus. I was once describing to a friend how my bipolar disorder had caused me so much pain that—at the risk of blasphemy—I said,

"I believe I have suffered more than Jesus. He only had to endure His pain for twenty-four hours—mine has been spread out over nearly thirty years of intermittent disillusionment, depression, mania, impulsiveness, anger, and loneliness."

She gave the most *shocking* reply: "He was! He was then and is NOW with you in any of your suffering! He suffers *with* you."

This statement blew me away, and became a huge impetus in my deciding to write a book about my mental health journey. If Jesus was, is, and will be in our suffering—actually suffering with us—then how could we ever feel that His Passion was in vain? His Passion is lived out daily in our struggles and brokenness, and His joys are shared in our revelations and hopes. These are gifts to us also—yesterday, today, and forever!

As I pray the rosary, sometimes I *spiritually* travel across time and support Jesus in his carrying of the cross or receiving of the lashes. I believe that, as I pray to Him, I *enter* His Passion and "am there for Him," to help Him endure His agonies, *as they were happening* 2,000 years ago. This may sound like a hokey metaphysical exercise, but I truly believe that if it is practiced in the imagination, it can enter into the timelessness of spirituality and become reality.

Spirituality is just that: of the Spirit, and the Spirit knows no time-boundaries; all possibilities are open. So I encourage you to use your imagination in prayer, and BE at the bedside of that loved one as he or she is dying, whether it be today, tomorrow, or twenty-five years ago. God wants us to spread Love—even across time.

* * * * * * * * * * * *

B. I once had the experience of working with a severely autistic and developmentally disabled Jewish child named Jason. He was so cognitively disabled that he couldn't feed himself or use the restroom without assistance. Usually, working with him in a school setting was boring and uncomfortable because he was so unresponsive.

But one day at school, I was with him in a small room and, after we played with some multi-colored blocks for a few minutes, I began to lightly stroke the top of his left hand. This eleven-year-old boy became calm and serene as my right hand stroked his left hand.

Suddenly, the whole world opened up in front of me, like flying over the edge of the Grand Canyon in a hang-glider. I could sense that the love and affection which I was giving to Jason *at that moment* was actually being given to a Nazi prison camp victim in 1944; that love was traveling across time. Or perhaps my loving attention to Jason was blessing a young person who had yet to be born, or easing stress and pain in some future dilemma of theirs as a teenager.

I could have been imagining all of this—and yes—it was happening *in* my imagination. But, to me, that doesn't make it any less REAL. God knows no boundaries, and any form of prayer is going to reach *whomever*, in God's good graces—if we pray earnestly and honestly.

* * * * * * * * * * * *

C. It was a new awakening for me one day, as I decided to pray a modified version of the T.E.R.M. rosary in the swimming pool. I had been listening to an author whose expertise is meditation and spiritual wholeness and I finally realized that the one and a half years that I've been praying the rosary have offered little time for quiet contemplation—quiet in the mind, that is. All those Hail Marys—were they really doing me any good? Were they truly "prayer" or just recitation? Most of the time my mind has either been on the mystery, or distracted with direct thoughts of Jesus and His life, not focused on Mother Mary.

If one is praying to Mary, shouldn't one's focus be on Mary? But I've been taught that we ought to be thinking about the mysteries while praying the Hail Mary.

So, I tried a few things different one day. I swam. Usually I walk for my T.E.R.M. rosaries. But that day it was a rhythmical stroke that accompanied me in my prayer. Then I thought, *How can I still have some structure, still have some familiar prayer, and yet have the "silence"?* I decided to spend a few moments praying about the mysteries: that day, the Sorrowful Mysteries, because it was a Friday; then I would pray an Our Father, a Hail Mary, and enter into silent contemplation, accompanied by a few occasional connections with Jesus.

It was amazing. By skipping nine out of ten Hail Marys and letting my mind rest, the Holy Spirit filled me with joy and hope, although I was praying the most unhappy mysteries of all—the Sorrowful Mysteries. My laps in the pool went by very quickly, as I felt freedom from worry about how far into the rosary I was, or how many Hail Marys I had prayed and how many I had left to go. And for the first time in many years of swimming off and on, I had no connection with how many laps I was swimming. This was a blessing in itself, because I had previously focused mostly on lap count. And that day I ended up swimming for fifteen minutes, and who knows how many laps. But I was focusing on the Passion of our Lord. My mind was uncluttered. My body flew through the water like an angel on the wing. It was pretty incredible!

Since this is not a chronological journal of my praying of the rosary, I do not know when the next entry about an event like this will appear, but I do know that this was a life-changer. This was more of a meditation on the rosary than the rosary itself, because I didn't pray the ten Hail Marys each time, but it was powerful. Thank You, God, for this new way of reaching toward You.

The Scourging at the Pillar

A. Many years ago, I heard the phrase "by His stripes we are healed," never realizing until years later that these "stripes" were the wounds Christ suffered during the scourging at the pillar. This form of torture is so pronounced because it covers such a large area of the body. In a certain sense, it may have meant that "nobody was covering His back"; Jesus was totally vulnerable and helpless. He even stated this on the cross: *"My God, my God, why have you abandoned me?"*

How often do we feel this way? The pain of the scourging in our lives comes raining down when we feel like *nobody's covering our back*. This is where the Holy Spirit comes in, to shield us from harm. Most often, the Holy Spirit shows up in the healing care of those we love. When we doubt ourselves into complaisance or think ourselves into a vicious cycle of negativity, the Spirit touches us through the loving touch of others.

We can all probably remember a time when we became ill and our mothers nursed us back to health. This is the Spirit at work, in practical, loving ways. And we offer the same care to others in a myriad of ways, if we are following our call.

The stripes that Jesus took were taken for us, in our sinfulness, in our loneliness, in our brokenness. Jesus truly took a beating in ways we will most likely never imagine—all in the process of becoming our Savior. The pain of the scourging is our pain, and our pain is surprisingly His!

* * * * * * * * * * * *

B. In the 2013 film "*12 Years a Slave*," a female slave is whipped so severely that her back looked like raw meat. She nearly died from the cruel treatment by her slave owner.

> Jesus' back must have looked similar to the slave's. "…by his wounds we were healed." (Isaiah 53:5) I'm amazed and humbled by how our Savior took on some of the worst of human pain for the sake of our redemption. I compare this to the millions of people today who suffer with back pain. It's as though they are taking on the scourging of Christ every day. They know how He felt. He knows how they feel. This mutuality can be comforting to one who is suffering with back pain. Knowing that Jesus understands the pain, the distress, the agony, the immobility—this can make it possible to go on, even into an unknown future with no relief in sight.
>
> We have a Savior who has experienced all pain, if not in His life, than by His unity with all people—in whatever pain they may have experienced or are experiencing. Jesus' divine empathy allows us to rest in the knowledge that we are never forgotten, and that He will always be with us, no matter what pain we encounter, whether in body, mind, heart, or spirit.

The Crowning with Thorns

A. Jesus, Savior of the world, was abused by persecutors who rammed a thorny crown onto His head. To me, this crown represents the pain that encircles our world, from the times of Christ and before, to the recent traumas of war, starvation, captivity, and hatred. All the suffering that *had* happened, *is* happening, and *will* happen can be symbolized by this piercing "crown" that encircled His head, indicating that all points of the world are affected by violence and hatred, and that suffering is universal. Jesus truly bore our pain in His Passion, suffering such intense pain that He now has what Cardinal Newman calls "an empathetic influence"; a true bearing of our pain now, in the present.

How can we go wrong with the Son of God on our side, empathizing with us, comforting and forgiving us, as we often stumble and bumble on our paths through life? I think back to tough times in my life and realize that Jesus was not merely figuratively *there for me*, but actually **there for me**, at that moment, in my mind, body, spirit, and heart!

For me, I now see how Mother Mary, Our Lady of Guadalupe, has been and is my advocate, my gentle powerful force, urging me in the direction of her son. And at times I wonder if the crown she wears in heaven represents the other side of the veil—the other side of death when we are to meet our God face-to-face. But, certainly, I see both Jesus' and Mary's crowns as "crowns of glory": Jesus as Redeemer and Mary as nurturer *of* the Redeemer. For without her saying "YES" to God's call, we would have no one through which to be redeemed.

The other side of the physical pain was the pain of humiliation and mockery that accompanied the crown. He was given a purple cloak to represent royalty and a reed in His hand to represent a scepter, but Jesus was being stung and lambasted, mockingly proclaimed as "the King of the Jews." The emotional agony and humiliation must have been unendurable, but Jesus endured it!

I tried to imagine Christ wearing a crown of thorns, just now, but my mind came up blank. Jesus needed only one crown—the one of His pain in suffering to redeem sins—and I see Him now as having outlived the thorns. Such a crown He no longer needs.

* * * * * * * * * * * *

B. Those who suffer from migraine headaches wear their own *crown of thorns*. I can't imagine the crushing pain of a migraine headache. Jesus knew this pain so well, in the crown of thorns rammed down on His head. He is a God who can bring comfort because He truly experienced suffering. This is an example to me that Christ's Passion was an over-all-time, redemptive experience. Jesus' suffering not only represents, but is in communion with any trials, any depressing times, any struggles we will ever face because, in His Passion, HE HAS BEEN THERE, He IS there, and He WILL BE there.

Among other tortures, Jesus wore His crown in utter humility, and humiliation. That was the point. Not only did He endure physical pain but the pain of humiliation and contempt. And for those who bear the burden of migraines: He is with you. You are not alone.

* * * * * * * * * * * *

C. Good Friday, 2015, while on my T.E.R.M. rosary walk: I plodded through the Agony in the Garden and re-experienced moments of Mel Gibson's film *The Passion of Christ* which I had watched the day before. It was the Crowning with Thorns—the third Sorrowful Mystery. In the movie, blood dripped down from Jesus' sacred head when they crammed the thorns down onto His skull. It was outrageous!

As has happened before while praying previous T.E.R.M. rosaries, I thought, momentarily, of how I relate to this agony. No, I do not have migraines and I have not undergone the humiliation and mocking which Jesus experienced. But I do have bipolar disorder. It is a disease of the brain (almost like "the crown") which can cause dramatic mood fluctuations, brain dysfunction, and behavioral disturbances. These are my layman's terms for a stupefying illness that came to me in the form of depression during my senior year in high school. It then exploded into a heightened manic state seven months later.

I mention in these pages that I once had an experience of enlightenment, in which I realized that Jesus was there with me in these (and many other) suffering times. This idea of His unity with me in my suffering was something I had never known before. And I have experienced this again: I know that I have not been alone in my bipolar struggles, and that Jesus has always been with me.

Also, in my devotion to Mary, I believe she has been at my side, especially during my relapse in 2008. I am especially devoted to her under the title Our Lady of Guadalupe, as impressed on the colorful card that I wrote about in the introduction to this book. I know she has been there to comfort me (as I've prayed the rosary and beyond) and to pray *for* me to the Father as a special advocate on my behalf. What a magnificent blessing to have Jesus and His mother on my side! My crown of thorns has been relieved many times by their influence.

* * * * * * * * * * * *

D. It occurred to me on my T.E.R.M. rosary walk one day that those who rammed the crown of thorns on Jesus' head had an "HRQ" (Highly Redeeming Quality) going on within them—that of CREATIVITY! They gave Him a crown to mock Him as a king; they gave Him a reed and put a royal purple cloak over Him—signs of royalty in those says. They did all this to demoralize and humiliate Him. How creative!

Isn't it ironic that sometimes the most creative people are the bullies, using their wit and skills to denigrate others, to make them feel less-than, to show hatred and ill-will? What if the bullies of these days put their efforts toward something good, such as comforting the injured and lifting up the weak? What if creativity were magnified in the positive sense: what if the atom bombs and grenades and other forms of destruction had not been created, and their resources had been put toward the good?

We can still do that! We can be a force for good and use our creativity to create life-giving actions and objects. Even though the torturers and bullies often have their way, it's not over yet!

The Carrying of the Cross

A. Splinters in the shoulder, knees crashing to cobble stone... what more pain did Jesus have to suffer? Jesus was allowed a cross bearer, Simon of Cyrene, so that He would live long enough to be nailed to the cross and suffer all the more. The cruelty, the humiliation, the absolute agony that Jesus went through—and all this for you and me!

And He asks us to carry our crosses, to plod along in our lives of stress and struggling. He strengthens us by being there in our troubles—truly BEING THERE! Jesus meant it when He said He would be with us always! He resides in our hearts, although we often forget He is present; He bears our crosses *with* us. He resides in our hands as we touch the world with our work and our affection. He sees through our eyes with compassion and love towards every single person, no matter the illness, disability, race, gender, or condition.

I know, truly, that Jesus has been there for me in my hours of stress and anxiety. He has propped up my cross, with all His experience of suffering. And He has been there to celebrate life with me, just as He celebrated with friends and family at the wedding at Cana. What a glorious example of living in the moment, to bear the cross of the sins of the world, right on to His crucifixion and eventual Resurrection. Thank You, Jesus!

* * * * * * * * * * * *

B. With all the depictions of the cross around us—around the neck, standing on the altar, hanging from the rear view mirror, marbleized on the church floor—it's still hard to understand what Jesus must have felt traveling that horrific trail to His crucifixion. How must Jesus have seen His life at that moment? He was bruised, torn, and bloodied, with no earthly future. Jesus' cross is the mystery—the Paschal Mystery—that brings life and death together into the promise of Life Everlasting.

* * * * * * * * * * * *

C. I have mentioned what I am about to expound on before, but allow me to share my story with further detail:

It was a conversation with a friend, a conversation that brought me to a new place. We were walking on a quiet city street, one sunny afternoon, when I began to share with her what I considered a personal blasphemy. She was intrigued and asked me to go on. I considered her a highly spiritual, traditional Catholic woman—maybe not the right person to tell, but I took the risk and said:

"I really don't believe Jesus suffered as much as I have."

She listened intently.

I went on: "I have suffered for over twenty-eight years with bipolar disorder—the strain, the loneliness, the hospitalizations, the depressions and manic bouts—if you count all that up, it adds up to be much more than twenty-four hours of excruciating pain. At least Jesus only had to suffer for one day. I've had all these years! He hasn't gone through what I've gone through!"

And with a light touch, like that of a butterfly landing on my shoulder, she said, "He did!"

I stopped on the pavement and looked at her in amazement.

"What you went through," she said. "He was there—He went through it with you."

I was shocked—not that I didn't believe—but because I knew it to be true. Jesus had carried that cross for me to Calvary *and* all the way through to that moment. It was one of the most humbling, ego-deflating moments of my life. Suddenly I realized that I was not alone—never alone—in my struggles! And Jesus still helps me bear my cross today. His example of tenacity and perseverance challenges me to wade through my minor struggles and forge through the major ones. It's amazing what a little conversation with a friend can do. It changed a whole viewpoint, my way of thinking, my whole heart-position, and brought me back to a spiritual reality that encourages hope and resiliency. This friend wanted to see growth in me, and make it stick. And it did.

The Crucifixion

A. While on my T.E.R.M. rosary walk, one cool September day, a Friday, I felt immediately compelled to move—as through spiritual transportation—and to BE THERE with Jesus as He was experiencing His Passion.

I was there, on the rock in the garden, with my arm around Him, then holding His hands. When He said, shaking, "I'm afraid," I responded with, "We (all of us, through time, who were and will be saved by Your Passion) are with You." He became quiet and continued to pray, sweating blood.

As I prayed the rest of the Sorrowful Mysteries, connecting with Jesus across time, taking his lashes, wearing His crown of thorns, carrying His cross (imagining actual times that I had suffered similar emotional experiences), I was nailed to the cross. I imagined my very good friend who is currently unemployed nailed to a cross, and me, pulling out the nails and bandaging his wounds; then him doing the same for me.

On this particular rosary walk, as I finished the fifth Sorrowful Mystery, the Crucifixion, having prayed it aloud (as I had done that whole T.E.R.M. rosary, on the private city park path near my home), I became silent. I continued to walk and suddenly thought about how my friend and I had come to one another's rescue. I thought, *relief and belief—we can give one another relief and belief.* Being a big fan of acronyms, I suddenly realized that a wonderful acronym had appeared:

G.R.A.B.

......Give
      Relief
           And
                  Belief

I was being called to give others **relief** from their suffering and the **belief** that they are loved by God supremely! And the words of comfort started to flow…

Give Relief and Belief…G.R.A.B.…

- ➢ GRAB to pull others off the ledge of despair…

- ➢ GRAB to hold others tight and show them your love and affection…

- ➢ GRAB others when they're about to make a huge mistake…

- ➢ GRAB them with the Holy Spirit that fills our souls…

- ➢ GRAB those we see in need and give them their fill…

- ➢ GRAB the opportunity to experience their goodness and praise God for the opportunity to serve…

I entered these words into my mini-notebook as I returned home from my walk. The act of entering fully into the Passion of Christ had stirred up a passion within me that I hadn't seen for a very long time. I'm so grateful for the T.E.R.M. rosary and for Mary's influence which makes these inspirations possible—and powerful!

* * * * * * * * * * * *

B. What did Mother Mary know? Did she know what was in store for her son, and for the world, as she saw her son being forced and prodded toward His crucifixion? Did she know that He was to rise on the third day and become the Redeemer of all mankind? Did she know she would see Him alive, after His death?

I sometimes wonder if she was as confused and frightened as everyone else at the bloody scene; and how powerless she must have felt, seeing her son, the Son of God, being violently escorted by angry crowds to His imminent demise. I imagine she was as shocked and overjoyed as anyone—if not more—to see her son alive once again. Did she know that she would see Him again? She was blessed but, yes, human. Thank God she had such faith to carry her through those three ugly days of waiting!

* * * * * * * * * * * *

C. Nailed to the cross…

After the torture of mind in the garden, the whip, the crown, the carrying of the cross, finally Jesus is held hostage. Nailed. Stationary. Stuck. Before, He could at least move around. Now He is fastened in place.

Jesus knew He would end up there, that He would be raised up on high, that He would not last through the day. He had given up His freedom. He had offered His body, mind, heart, and soul to His father. It must have been a relief, in a way, to have reached His destination, the one He had predicted so many times. He hung, gasping, for our sins, and He bore them, and finally breathed His last.

So why do Catholics have Christ Crucified hanging from their necks and on their rosaries? Why? Because the story didn't end there. In a strangely ironic way, it is a sign of HOPE that the story did not end there, with Jesus on the cross; it is a reminder that He was to fulfill the prophecy by rising on the third day.

Not only is the crucifix a reminder that Jesus suffered for our sins and that He met His death there, but that His death meant our rising to new life, for, as he died and rose, we did too.

The crucifix…a sign of the Paschal Mystery…Christ has died, Christ has risen, Christ will come again! This IS *the sign of the cross!*

Chapter 7

The Glorious Mysteries

Sunday—The Glorious Mysteries

The Resurrection, The Ascension,
The Descent of the Holy Spirit, The Assumption of Mary,
and The Coronation of Mary

The Resurrection

A. The joy of it—Jesus conquering death! It brings me into a place of great JOY to imagine Jesus rising from the dead to bring us salvation! And yet His glorified body was still showing the holes in His hands, feet, and side. How could He not be in pain? Because a spiritual body is not a mortal body. It may seem to take on the form of the previous reality, but no longer do His wounds bleed. Jesus had already shed His blood—He will never die again.

What more could anyone have given us than three years of passionate proclamation, an excruciating passion and death, and the opportunity for everlasting life? To have Jesus IN OUR SUFFERING each day, as we struggle along our paths, loving us, bringing us into His Passion, empathizing with us—these are some of the graces of Jesus Christ.

He freely chose to suffer all that. He did not have to, but He did. And He does. The Resurrection IS the pivot-point for our Christian lives on earth. *It is the middle of the beginning of the end*; our end, in movement toward a life of glory in heaven with Him.

* * * * * * * * * * * * *

B. Luke 24:13–35 speaks of Jesus meeting two men on the road to Emmaus, soon after His Resurrection. They were prevented from knowing His true identity until He broke bread with them and gave the blessing: "With that their eyes were opened and they recognized him, but he vanished from their sight." Wow! God has worked wonders within me, on reading this verse!

While on the way to choir the other night, I purposefully didn't turn on the radio or cassette player because I wanted to have a heart-to-heart talk with my Savior. I was deeply struggling with the whole idea of the Eucharist, and why we as Catholics put such emphasis on it; I wondered if it was truly His body and blood; and if so, why it had to be so; and why must we eat His body and drink His blood?

Now, my personal reflection is that the bread (which becomes His body) represents Jesus' life, and the wine (which becomes His blood) represents His suffering, and as these elements are raised by the priest, they represent His Resurrection.

But just as I read from Luke 24:31 recently, it occurred to me that THIS is how we "recognize Him"! We are given actual signs, manifestations of His Presence, when the bread and wine BECOME His body and blood. We recognize the significance of His life, death, and Resurrection in the breaking of the bread. We see and experience Jesus for who He was, is, and will be, because we have received His body and blood and are truly united with Him.

THIS is the significance I see in the Emmaus story, this post-Resurrection account of two men coming to believe in the glory and majesty of God through just a simple act of gratitude and generosity: Jesus recognized in the breaking of the bread.

In the Breaking of the Bread

How do we recognize the Presence of the Lord?
How do we sense *the terrible swift sword*?
And how do we hear him in His Holy Word?
~In the breaking of the bread~

We didn't see Him while walking on dusty roads
and didn't recognize Him as we slowly strode;
only to find Him at the table, lifting the load
~In the breaking of the bread~

Each loaf broken into many parts
for us to receive new life—right from the start.
In His presence we sense a brilliant work of art
~In the breaking of the bread~

Jesus becomes visible in the preparation,
not to leave us in doubt, hatred, and separation
but loving us in each and every situation
~In the breaking of the bread~

When it becomes real to us all
we come together as one, in The Call
no longer to feel frail or weak or small
~In the breaking of the bread~

We proclaim "He is risen indeed!"
For Him to meet every dashed and forgotten need
and moving us, in grace, with Him in the lead
~In the breaking of the bread~

Grace handed to us by one another
by every person—whether sister, friend, or brother
in glory, honor and praise—there is no other
~In the breaking of the bread~

We call Jesus Lord—we call Him friend.
He sees us struggle, yet sees us through to the end
by giving us the grace to heal and time to mend
~In the breaking of the bread~

* * * * * * * * * * * * *

C. Easter Sunday. The Holy Saturday liturgy was celebrated the previous night. I had experienced a dark church steadily come to life as the light was spread, from a single candle—candle to candle—representing the light of Christ moving from person to person. The Holy Spirit was palpable in this sanctified service where eight people were baptized, four children and four adults. These new members of the Church were fully immersed three times: *in the name of the Father, and of the Son, and of the Holy Spirit*, bringing them to a new life in Christ.

I had never witnessed full immersion before. It reminded me of the old preacher from the country church, dunking the new believers in the river. It was not a mere trickling of a little water over the head! Even the babies went fully under three times. It was exhilarating and joyful!

Praise You, Jesus, for all You went through for us; the cleansing Blood of the Lamb washing away sin through baptism. It's so humbling when I truly realize the sacrifice You made for me—for us! I adore You in Your magnificence. Thank You for Your great glory!

The Ascension

A. "The Homecoming" was the name of a 1970s film about a family awaiting the Christmas Eve arrival of their father who had been caught in a blizzard while trying to return from a far-off destination. The name of the family? The Waltons. This was the pilot movie for the series that ran for so many years on TV.

Why does this come up in my memory? Because the Ascension was *Jesus' homecoming*, after a long, hard trek here on earth, having spread His message of the Good News and being crucified to save us from our sins. This was His time to return to His home, heaven, and to once again "sit at the right hand of the Father."

Jesus left saying that He would send One to be with us always: the Holy Spirit. I believe that He was saying, "Carry on; carry on with what I started. Carry on with the skills I taught you. Carry on with loving one another as I have loved you!"

The apostles and the rest of Jesus' followers were charged with the responsibility and the joy of spreading the Word of God, and it seems they believed that He would return in their day and age. But the Holy Spirit has been our guide and hope (as the Holy Spirit was theirs), and we too continue to wait for Jesus' second coming. Many people have proclaimed that when Jesus said "the time is at hand," it meant He would be coming very soon.

"But doesn't everyone go to heaven?" some might ask. I don't know. My duty is to live out THIS life with integrity and authenticity, and I let God do the rest. As long as I live out my calling, and assist others with gifts of compassion, love, and hope along their paths, I believe I will have done my part.

Yes, I want to go to heaven, and I believe I will go to heaven, but KNOWING for certain that I will go to heaven is left up to the Father. So I do not worry too much about it. Yes, I want a homecoming like Jesus had; not to be seated at the right hand of the Father, but to rest my soul in a place of spiritual bliss.

I could make this a goal, I could own this dream, but again, it is up to God to make it a reality because I am a mere mortal, a sinner who bows at the feet of my God, praying, "Lord, I am not worthy that You should enter under my roof, but only say the Word and my soul shall be healed." Amen. Amen.

* * * * * * * * * * * *

B. Did Jesus go up to heaven to live in eternal bliss? Well, if He is ever-present with us, in our struggles, in our downfalls, in our triumphs and joys, then He must be playing an ACTIVE role in our lives.

I believe Jesus suffers along with us when we are experiencing troubles. He is not only *an on-time God*, but an *all-the-time*

God. At the time of His ascension, an angel said that He would come back the same way He went up, but didn't say what He'd be doing in between. I imagine that He is pretty busy with being our Savior. He did send the Holy Spirit to be our Advocate, but there is nothing like the "real thing," the REAL PRESENCE of Jesus in our lives.

Pentecost: The Descent of the Holy Spirit

A. At Pentecost, Jesus breathed on the apostles and the Holy Spirit descended upon them. Their hearts were filled with joy. What happened when Jesus "said the blessing" at the Last Supper, establishing the Eucharist (which translated means *thanksgiving*)? He expressed *gratitude*. Why do we "say grace" before a meal? We are expressing *gratitude*.

The Holy Spirit and gratitude are very close partners. For instance, when the dove came down from heaven at Jesus' baptism, God said, "You are my beloved Son in whom I am well pleased." Was the Father grateful to Jesus for all the blood, sweat, and tears He had put forth in His thirty years of preparing for that moment? And Jesus showed gratitude to His father for blessing Him with the waters of baptism.

From the Holy Spirit flows the river of life. The water cannot flow without gratitude. We may go along in our lives thinking we're so great, that we're succeeding all by ourselves. But without gratitude—a gift from the Holy Spirit—the "waters" have no banks to contain them and they flood the plains with ingratitude. We can lose focus on the reality that we do not "do it ourselves." God does!

The gift of Gratitude, buttressed by Faith and Peace, creates an atmosphere of love, forgiveness, hope, and grace that can overcome any difficulty, any doubt, any breach of trust, any pain. Saint Paul said, "In all things give thanks." This is so important to remember, but do we? I can see giving thanks for the "good" things, but giving thanks for the "bad"?

I have a colleague who recently told me she had found her dream job; but before she could start it, she totaled her car, making it impossible for her to get to work. But in losing this possibility, she realized that she could go back to school and better her future by getting an education. Without the car wreck, she would not have gone back to school, or even thought she could have. Her testing ground became her fertile soil. Sometimes you have to lose in order to win! She had the *gift of Gratitude* and was grateful for her mishap because it brought her to higher ground.

The Holy Spirit is always with us, in us; and when we respond with gratitude, we are given more. It's called *the law of attraction*—like attracts like. What we think about, what we give thanks for, moves toward us, and we toward it. In writing this book, I am already thanking God for its completion because I know God can take my dream and make it a reality. I am grateful that my book is on the way—in essence, it IS already published!

Where is the Holy Spirit, this Third Person of the Trinity, calling you to be grateful in your life?

* * * * * * * * * * * *

B. How many times has the Holy Spirit come into your life at just the right time? I had an amazing experience of being blessed by the Holy Spirit recently. I was about to give a ten-minute talk on *kenosis*, a process of emptying the self, as Philippians says Jesus did, Chapter 2:7: "…he emptied himself, taking the form of a slave…"

I had planned on using these verses in my talk, but moments before it would begin, the moderator read this whole reading, making my speech a matter of redundancy if I were to present it as I had planned. What to do? Then I remembered that we were to speak from our own experience about a specific topic. I thought, *what type of emptying the self can I describe to get my point across about* kenosis?

Suddenly, it hit me. It was so obvious! I have struggled with bipolar disorder for over thirty years, and the humility and humiliation I have experienced in my many encounters with manic and depressive episodes gave exposure to *kenosis* in a very descriptive and personal way. So I delivered my piece.

Afterwards, five people came up to me to speak of a friend or loved one who struggled with the same illness. Wow! I am a speaker, yet bipolar disorder had been at the bottom of my list of topics which I wanted to speak on. Yet through the response I received, it became apparent that there is a hunger to learn more about bipolarity. So I decided, with the guidance of my wife, Sandra, to reconfigure our consulting business to focus on bipolar disorder. My passion for the topic arose like a dolphin catching air and we are on the way to revamping the program. The Holy Spirit is at work in a big way!

* * * * * * * * * * * *

C. Does the Holy Spirit come down to us when we pray for guidance, or is He already in our hearts, just waiting to be set free? I have often wondered this. What do *you* think? I remember walking out of a church on Pentecost Sunday years ago because I heard the priest use this "come down" language. I found it ridiculous and even scandalous. I was in somewhat of an extreme mood at the time, but my heart was in the right place. If we were offered the Spirit at baptism and Confirmation, then why would we even *think* we have to call Him down from above? He's already here!

The Glorious Mysteries

* * * * * * * * * * * *

D. Once, on a sunny, ten degree Sunday morning in Wisconsin, I went for a walk, praying the Glorious Mysteries. I got to the third, the Descent of the Holy Spirit, and began the Hail Marys. I found myself deeply thinking, nearly speaking to Jesus, "Thank You for sending the Holy Spirit; thank You for the Spirit within us; thank You for the Spirit moving out of us; thank You for the Spirit all around us—everywhere!"

In the 1977 film *Star Wars*, there was a positive spiritual presence that linked all things together called "The Force." The movie was filled with battles between good and evil. Yoda, a leader of "the good guys," the Jedi Knights, led by sensing the movements of "The Force," and the Jedi Knights were victorious because of his leadership. It was enlightening and encouraging to experience this depiction of spirituality in a secular film. Personally, I liken "The Force" to the Holy Spirit, that Third Person of the Trinity who unifies Christians spiritually.

The Assumption of Mary

A. Praying this mystery recently, I found myself in deep admiration for Mother Mary.

> Then it occurred to me that my mom has represented Mother Mary all my life. She has held my hand in times of struggle, laughed with me in times of jubilation, and counseled me in times of confusion. *This must be how Mother Mary is and has been active in my life*, I've thought to myself.

> I had never imagined Mother Mary as funny before. But she must be laughing with me at the most hilarious moments of

my life. And how close she is to me; always there whether I am happy or sad, or somewhere in between, just like my mom.

* * * * * * * * * * *

B. The Church teaches us that the Assumption was when Mary, the Mother of Jesus, was taken up to heaven, body and soul. This dogma states that her body was "uncorrupted," that it did not decay. This mystery shows how Mary is revered for being the Mother of God, and what grace she was given at the end of her life to be able to be "assumed" into heaven.

In praying the numerous Hail Marys as part of the T.E.R.M. rosary, we give her honor through repetition of these sacred words. In my heart, as Our Lady of Guadalupe, Mary has a special place. I realize that she has played a pivotal role in protecting me, and seeing that I stay in touch with her son, Jesus.

What a joy it is to know that I can come to her anytime, or in praying the T.E.R.M. rosary, for strength. She is the Mother of our Lord and she has such a prominent place in salvation history. Mary raised Jesus with Joseph, in Nazareth; she prompted Jesus to perform His first miracle (turning water into wine at the wedding at Cana); she stood before Him as He suffered on the cross. Mary was there for Jesus from beginning to end. She is to be highly revered. No other woman could ever be called *the Mother of God*. She is special!

The Coronation of Mary

A. During my T.E.R.M. rosary walk one sunny August afternoon, while praying the Glorious Mystery of the Coronation of Mary, I began to wonder what Mother Mary *really* looks like. I thought of the Our Lady of Guadalupe card that I found in August of 2008, and tried to picture her with brown skin and a green cloak. All I could imagine was the image on the multi-colored card in my pocket, not a real person.

So, I thought of taking magazines and clipping out a face and creating clothes, and pasting it to a page, creating an image of Mother Mary. Then I realized that all those faces in the magazines are the "pretty people," those seen in our society as enticing and enviable.

Suddenly, a strange thought occurred to me. "What if, when I get to heaven and meet Jesus and Mary, I recognized them, as if I had known them and seen them all my life?"

Then my thoughts took me further, and moved into a teachable moment. I imagined that EVERY woman or girl I see IS Mary, and that EVERY man or boy I see IS Jesus! That when God said we are His children, He meant we are to treat all as though they ARE Christ, and to see men as Jesus and women as His mother; which, for me, puts "love thy neighbor" into perspective. How could I not love those whom I see as "Mary"? She is my spiritual mother. I pray her rosary almost every day in love and humility. And how could I not love those whom I see as "Christ"? He *is* the one who died for my sins and gave me everlasting life.

This was a very edifying *and* sobering reflection: to see the faces of Mary and Jesus in ALL those I encounter! This image, this redistribution of thought and imagination, has given me new vigor. I can now see Mother Mary having the crown placed upon her head. She is everywhere! I can see her beauty, her diversity, her strength, in all the girls and women I see, all the time.

And I can see Jesus speaking to the multitudes and holding up bread and wine, because His face is everywhere! I no longer have to search for the Suffering Servant; He is in every male face around me, even in the mirror each morning. What a fresh perspective, and an invigorating idea: to envision my Jesus and His mother constantly, faces of familiarity, faces of joy.

* * * * * * * * * * * *

B. Have you ever wondered why Mary had on her head "a crown of twelve stars"? I once thought it represented the twelve apostles, or the twelve tribes of Israel.

   But on one T.E.R.M. rosary walk, it occurred to me that since Mary is with us every minute of every day, the twelve stars can represent the daytime hours. Mary is with us every day, to guide us, to lead us toward her son, to comfort us in times of need, to accompany us along paths of joy and sorrow. She is right here, in each heart, loving us.

   I am thankful that Our Lady gave us the rosary to help us focus on her son's life and to better live our lives. It is an honor to pray *through* her to Jesus, and a million blessings to have spent time relishing His life.

* * * * * * * * * * * *

C. Mother Mary is said to have been seen many times in the 20th century in visions known as "apparitions." At Fatima, she gave a message of warning and even dread if we didn't change our ways and move toward Jesus' ways. She has even been known as Our Lady of Sorrows; not merely grieving over her son's sufferings, but over the evils and destruction of hatred and war.

   But there is an apparition that touches my heart especially deeply, which I have mentioned throughout this book: the apparitions of Our Lady of Guadalupe, who was seen by a simple farmer, named Juan Diego, near Mexico City in AD 1531. There, Mary wore a starry green robe, and was "clothed with the sun" which shone around her body.

How do I know this? Because this image was imprinted on Juan Diego's *tilma*, an apron-like garment which he was wearing when our Lady appeared to him. This *tilma* still exists today and is encased in glass at the Basilica of Our Lady of Guadalupe in Mexico City. My wife, Sandra, and I took a pilgrimage there to see the blessed *tilma* in December of 2009. It was amazing to see the garment that, when it was woven, should only have lasted twenty years—and there it still is, five hundred years later.

Mary had a simple message of love and hope, different than the ominous message of Fatima. She was dressed in native clothing, had the appearance of a young native woman, and was pregnant with Jesus, which was signified by the black sash she had around her waist.

I like to reverently say: "To me, Lady of Guadalupe, you are not only the 'Lady of Sorrows,' but the mother of 'bringing Christ to Life,' expressed in your Holy Rosary, in your prayers to God the Father for us, in your glorious bearing of our Savior, the Bringer of salvation to the world!"

* * * * * * * * * * * *

D. In AD 1531, Our Lady presented herself as a pregnant young Indian woman to Juan Diego near what was to become Mexico City. *Pregnant* is the word I want you to focus on for a moment. Jesus was WITHIN her, unlike all the other apparitions of Mary. And if Jesus was WITHIN her, in a certain sense, she hasn't gone through all the pain and joy of having her son in her life, as we look back at salvation history. She is like us, waiting, loving, praying; Our Lady is a living example of how to approach life.

Have you ever seen a depiction of Our Lady of Guadalupe? I have seen the actual *tilma* that her image was impressed upon. She is serene. She is thoughtful. She is looking lovingly to the right, with hands together, fingers pointing upward—the classic Marian posture. She is in waiting; waiting prayerfully to bear the light of the world to us all. And she exemplifies how we need to be: waiting, prayerfully, for our lives to unfold.

I imagine Mary as being an active woman. Just look at how she took care of her cousin Elizabeth when both of them were pregnant, waiting on her every need; another example of how *goodness brings action*. How many times has Mary appeared on earth after her assumption? Lourdes, Fatima, Guadalupe, and so many other apparitions. She appeared in different garb to separate cultures and times, having a particular message for those she encountered. This is why the Aztecs came to Christianity by the millions in the mid-1500s. They could relate to her, for she chose to appear as a native, as one of them. And she relates to us in our struggles, in our pain, in our hope, and in our joy. We truly have a mother who understands!

* * * * * * * * * * * *

E. I find it interesting that the rosary starts with the scene in which Mother Mary says "yes" to God at the Annunciation, and it ends with God saying "YES" to her, as the crown is placed upon her head.

Section III
Basics of the Rosary

Chapter 8
The Basics of the Rosary

The Holy Rosary dates back to AD 1214, when Saint Dominic was given the rosary from the Blessed Virgin as a means of converting the Albigensians and other sinners. It was originally comprised of the Joyful, Sorrowful, and Glorious Mysteries. Then, in 2002, Pope John Paul II instituted the five Luminous Mysteries. These four sets of mysteries are the foundation of the T.E.R.M. rosary. From here, the T.E.R.M. rosary is built.

How to Pray the Rosary

The rosary begins with "the Sign of the Cross":

In the name of the Father, (right hand touches the forehead)
and of the Son, (touch the heart)
and of the Holy (touch the left shoulder)
Spirit, (touch the right shoulder)
Amen. (hands come together in front)

Particulars of the Rosary

1. Recite the *Apostles' Creed* (holding the crucifix)
2. Pray an *Our Father* (holding first bead)
3. Pray three *Hail Mary*s (one bead for each)
4. Pray a *Glory Be* (between beads), and announce the first mystery (see mysteries schedule)
5. Pray an *Our Father*
6. Pray ten *Hail Mary*s, while meditating on a particular mystery
7. Pray a *Glory Be*
8. Announce the second mystery, then pray an *Our Father*. Repeat steps 6 and 7, continuing the third, fourth, and fifth mysteries in the same manner.

After the rosary, pray the *Hail Holy Queen* prayer:

> Hail Holy Queen, Mother of Mercy, our life, our sweetness, and our hope. To thee do we cry, poor banished children of Eve; to thee do we send up our sighs, mourning and weeping in this vale of tears. Turn then, most gracious advocate, thine eyes of mercy toward us, and after this our exile, show unto us the blessed fruit of thy womb, Jesus. O clement, O loving, O sweet Virgin Mary!

Optional: After each decade (ten Hail Marys), pray the following prayer, as requested by the Blessed Virgin at Fatima:

> O my Jesus, forgive us our sins, save us from the fires of hell; lead all souls to heaven, especially those who are in most need of Thy mercy.

End with the sign of the cross.

Prayers of the Rosary

Apostles' Creed

I believe in God, the Father Almighty,
Creator of heaven and earth;
and in Jesus Christ, His Only Son, our Lord,
who was conceived by the Holy Spirit,
born of the Virgin Mary,
suffered under Pontius Pilot,
was crucified, died, and was buried.
He descended into hell.
On the third day, He rose again from the dead;
He ascended into heaven and sits
at the right hand of God, the Father Almighty;
from thence He shall come to judge the
living and the dead.
I believe in the Holy Spirit,
the Holy Catholic Church,
the Communion of Saints,
the forgiveness of sins,
the resurrection of the body,
and life everlasting.
Amen.

Glory Be

Glory be to the Father, and to the Son, and to the
Holy Spirit, as it was in the beginning, is now
and ever shall be, world without end. Amen.

Our Father (The Lord's Prayer)

Our Father, who art in heaven,
hallowed be Thy name.
Thy kingdom come, Thy will be done,
on earth, as it is in heaven.
Give us this day our daily bread,
and forgive us our trespasses
as we forgive those who trespass against us.
And lead us not into temptation,
but deliver us from evil.
Amen.

(Optional) For Thine is the kingdom,
and the power, and the glory, now and forever.
Amen.

Hail Mary

Hail Mary, full of grace,
the Lord is with thee.
Blessed art thou among women
and blessed is the fruit of thy womb, Jesus.
Holy Mary, Mother of God,
pray for us sinners, now and at the hour
of our death.
Amen.

Enhanced Hail Mary

Hail Mary, full of grace,
the Lord is with thee.
Blessed art thou among women
and blessed is the fruit of thy womb, Jesus.
Holy Mary, Mother of God,
pray for us sinners,
and hold us in thy loving arms,
now and at the time of our deaths,
and walk us, with Jesus,
through the waiting gates of heaven.
Amen.

Author's Personal Prayer to Our Lady

Oh, Mother Mary, you are the advocate to bring
me to the throne of your son, Jesus Christ,
and for that I thank you.

I encourage you to incorporate the T.E.R.M. mysteries into your rosary devotion. Or, if you do not pray the rosary, I encourage you to grow spiritually by meditating on five mysteries each day and in respective reflections during your time of prayer. Visualize the scenes that depict fifteen additional scenes from Jesus' revered life, which allows for all thirty-five mysteries to be prayed each week. God bless you in your exploration of the T.E.R.M. rosary, and peace be with you.

Sincerely,
Rich Melcher

About the author

In March of 1982, Rich Melcher picked up a pen and an eighty-page theme book and wrote, "I write today not knowing if I will continue this journal in the future, but today I will write." Thousands of pages later, Rich is still writing, not only in his journal; he is currently the author of six books.

His works include *Just a Little Somethin'*, a 365-day personal development reader; a bipolar memoir entitled *Discerning Bipolar Grace*; and *Soul In Motion*, a book of selected poems. Rich rounds out his diverse topics with his first young adult novel, *A Work In Progress*, which is about Kuna, an urban youth living in Baltimore who discovers a hidden ethics code in which the next integrity clue can only be revealed if the previous ones are lived out in real life.

In 1982, Rich was introduced to the power of the rosary by a friend who prayed it devoutly, which planted a seed in him that would sprout in 2008, leading to the writing of *Journey with the Expanded Rosary*. This publication has opened the door for him to continue writing spiritual works, especially since spirituality had been the subject matter in many of his poetic endeavors.

Rich is also a speaker, an actor, and a worker in the mental health field. Since he lives with the challenges of bipolar disorder, he spreads the word of "the discovery of recovery" and how it has played a part in his life. He lives with his wife Sandra, who, among other things, is a mental health advocate. They reside in Milwaukee, Wisconsin.

 **About Leonine Publishers**

Leonine Publishers LLC makes fine Catholic literature available to Catholics throughout the English-speaking world. Leonine Publishers offers an innovative "hybrid" approach to book publication that helps authors as well as readers. Please visit our web site at www.leoninepublishers.com to learn more about us. Browse our online bookstore to find more solid Catholic titles to uplift, challenge, and inspire.

Our patron and namesake is Pope Leo XIII, a prudent, yet uncompromising pope during the stormy years at the close of the 19th century. Please join us as we ask his intercession for our family of readers and authors.

Do you have a book inside you? Visit our web site today. Leonine Publishers accepts manuscripts from Catholic authors like you. If your book is selected for publication, you will have an active part in the production process. This book is an example of our growing selection of literature for the busy Catholic reader of the 21st century.

www.leoninepublishers.com

www.ingramcontent.com/pod-product-compliance
Lightning Source LLC
Chambersburg PA
CBHW022107040426
42451CB00007B/159